RODUCED BY FAITH

DeVON FRANKLIN
PRODUCED BY FAITH
ENJOY REAL SUCCESS WITHOUT LOSING YOUR TRUE SELF

WITH TIM VANDEHEY

HOWARD BOOKS
A Division of Simon & Schuster, Inc.
New York Nashville London Toronto Sydney

Howard Books
A Division of Simon & Schuster, Inc.
1230 Avenue of the Americas
New York, NY 10020

First Howard Books hardcover edition May 2011

HOWARD and colophon are trademarks of Simon & Schuster, Inc.

For information about special discounts for bulk purchases, please contact Simon & Schuster Special Sales at 1-866-506-1949 or business@simonandschuster.com.

The Simon & Schuster Speakers Bureau can bring authors to your live event. For more information or to book an event, contact the Simon & Schuster Speakers Bureau at 1-866-248-3049 or visit our website at www.simonspeakers.com.

Designed by Davina Mock-Maniscalco

Manufactured in the United States of America

10 9 8 7 6 5 4 3 2 1

Library of Congress Cataloging-in-Publication Data
Franklin, DeVon.
Produced by faith: enjoy real success without losing your true self /
DeVon Franklin with Tim Vandehey.
   p. cm.
Includes bibliographical references.
1. Success—Religious aspects—Christianity.
2. Motion picture industry—Miscellanea. I. Vandehey, Tim. II. Title.
BV4598.3.F73 2011
248.4'86732—dc22
2010045978

ISBN 978-1-4391-7103-5
ISBN 978-4516-1270-7 (ebook)

This book is dedicated
to the memory of
my father, Donald Ray Franklin I;
my grandparents, Anita and James Camell;
and my great-grandparents, Ida and Percival Phillips.

I also dedicate this book to all of you
who have struggled with holding on to your faith.
This is one of life's most challenging pursuits.
I understand you, and I applaud you for not giving up hope.
This is my tribute to you.

CONTENTS

PART TWO: PRODUCTION

Scanning book cover:

Scan the cover
of this book with WiMO

to watch a message from DeVon Franklin right on your Smartphone.

Also, each chapter is accompanied
by a video introduction.

When you see a code, simply scan it with the free WiMO app
to unlock exclusive video content from DeVon.

Example chapter code:

Scanning chapter code
with the WIMO App:

SCAN THIS CODE WITH
THE WIMO MOBILE APP

WiMO ENABLED

WiMO ENABLED

PREFACE

Trust in the Lord with all your heart,
And lean not on your own understanding;
In all your ways acknowledge Him,
And He shall direct your paths.
—Proverbs 3:5–6 NKJV

I was deep in the heart of Beijing, People's Republic of China, in the summer of 2009. For the first time in my career, I was the lead studio executive on a feature film—the remake of *The Karate Kid*, starring Jackie Chan and Jaden Smith, son of actor Will Smith.

It's important to understand that Beijing—the ancient capital of China—is *huge*. The urban area alone contains about 13 million residents; that's four cities of Los Angeles. Beijing is also complex on a Byzantine scale, and with the producers, entire crew, and cast there, we had ventured far

1

into some of the oldest parts of the city, into ancient neighborhoods called *hutongs* where the living style was more communal and we could find the character and feel we were looking for.

Getting cast, crew, and equipment there was a major undertaking, the shots were taking a long, long time to set up and complete, and as I stood there, we were running out of daylight.

Sunset is usually panic time for a film crew. Unless you're shooting night scenes, you try to work in every last shot you can, using reflectors to capture every last bit of natural light. The crew was working as quickly as they could to maximize what was a very expensive day of production. But I had other concerns. I glanced at my watch, shot a look at the disappearing sun, and knew that even though I was the sole representative for Columbia Pictures on set, I had to leave.

I had no choice. That is, I didn't *give myself* a choice.

Fortunately, the producers knew that I would be making my way back to the hotel. It wasn't a surprise to anybody. I pulled one of the production assistants aside, told him I would be catching a taxi, left the production in the capable hands of the producers and director, and disappeared into the streets of Beijing. It was an act that might have been ridiculed if I hadn't set a precedent years before and remained committed to it. Leaving set on the first movie you're running—shooting halfway around the world—isn't advisable if you want a long prosperous career in Hollywood.

But I didn't lose my job.

In fact, my departure didn't make a ripple in the day's shoot. I was able to attend to something infinitely more important: keeping a promise to God that I made many years before.

I was born thirty-two years ago and raised as a Seventh-day Adventist. Among other things, that means I celebrate the Sabbath. So from sunset on Friday to sunset on Saturday, I unplug from my hectic life as a Columbia film executive. No work. I don't check e-mail or roll calls. I break the fourth commandment of the movie business— *Thou shalt never turn off thy BlackBerry*—and turn off my BlackBerry.

The Sabbath is my time with the Lord, my time to unwind from the pressures of work, heal, and reflect on the many blessings in my life and the career path that has led me here. On Friday nights I study my Bible, pray, spend quiet hours in communion with God, and make plans with family for church and fellowship on Saturday.

Unless I happen to be in Beijing. In that case, I'll read Scripture, watch the incredible metropolis slowly come to life, and pray that the dailies look good. Normally I would go to church, but in China most of the Christian churches are underground and I had no idea how to go about finding them. So I settled for reading the Bible and spending time in private communion with God—my own personal church in the midst of one of the world's busiest cities.

The next morning, I decided that didn't want to spend the entire Sabbath in my hotel room. I ended up going to a park right outside the Olympic Village where I could sit under God's sky, watch the birds, listen to gospel music, and read the Word. As I was going through Romans, the idea came to me for this book. Just like that, clear as day.

* * *

YOU MAY FIND IT impossible that a Hollywood studio executive is also a devout Christian. But it's not a contradiction. In reality, my business is not very different from your own. There are opportunities, politics, unspoken expectations, and a set of rules for advancement that are very different from the Lord's rules. No matter what line of work you find yourself in, you may feel that being a Christian is holding you back. You may feel caught between a rock and a hard place. On one hand, if you don't toe the company line and put your career first, can you still call yourself a company man or woman? On the other, if you ignore the Word and set aside the precepts of your faith when it's convenient, can you still call yourself a Christian? Sometimes, it feels like we're walking on a tightrope and below us there's no net, just a big, dark abyss.

I've got great news. I've found that it is possible to put Christ first and have a thriving career. In fact, I believe it's necessary. My favorite scripture is Philippians 4:13, "I can do all things through Christ who strengthens me." God is our strength; his love, demonstrated through us, can move mountains and change hearts. Being a Christian is actually a *competitive edge* . . . provided that you place your faith first above even your professional aspirations. Even if in the past you've compromised and slid partway down that slippery slope, it's still possible to find your way back. If I have learned anything, it's this:

> *To get where you want to go, you first have to become the person God wants you to be.*

I know writing this book is definitely part of my journey to become who God wants me to be. Some would probably say I'm crazy. The common practice when you're in business is that you write a book after you've either reached your goal and accumulated some power and prominence or left your industry altogether. I'm in neither place. I'm just like most of the people reading this book: still climbing the corporate ladder and/or right in the middle of my career pursuit. Yet I believe God has called me right now to share my unique experiences and this urgent message with you, so I must be obedient to his will.

The message? During my time in the film industry, I have put my faith front and center for everyone to see. It's my experience that people handle the intersection of faith and career in one of two ways. Some conceal their beliefs at the workplace, dumping their Christian principles on the kitchen table like a spare set of keys when they leave the house in the morning. Others refuse the command to be "in the world but not of the world" and work only in environments run by and for other Christians.

Both approaches are problematic. If we lock our faith in the closet from nine to five because we're afraid of ridicule or questions about our loyalty, what governs our choices in climbing the career ladder? Will we lie, cheat others, or stab people in the back, then go home at the end of the day and put on our "I'm a Christian" clothes again? Plenty of people do exactly that because they fear that if they go public with their faith at work, they will be perceived as weak, divisive, or unwilling to do whatever it takes to succeed. But if we make such a choice, what does that say about our faith?

On the other hand, as believers we sometimes shun the secular world and limit our job prospects to a select group of potential employers or industries that we believe will be Christian friendly. But by doing so, we can lock ourselves in an echo chamber of ideas and beliefs just like our own, so we never really stretch or grow. Sometimes, we come to regard the world outside our bubble as the enemy.

When some Christians learn that I've worked in entertainment for over ten years, I can feel them take a mental step backward, as if they feel I'm sleeping with the enemy. I'm not offended; to many Christians, Hollywood is a modern-day Sodom and Gomorrah. This business is probably the last place most people expect to find a young Christian visibly and vocally expressing his faith while progressing in his career. But the truth is that not only has relying on my faith not harmed my career prospects, it has actually enhanced them.

Thrilling opportunities to work with the most dynamic people in the world have come my way precisely *because* I have been uncompromising about my Christian principles and making service to God the centerpiece of my work. Over the course of my career I have developed a set of guiding principles that I live by:

- God's will has priority over mine.
- Commit to the process of success that God has planned for me, no matter how long it takes.
- God has the authority to put my ambition in check.

- Strive to let the love of Christ be apparent in everything I do.

- Do not allow sin to reside in any area of my life. If I allow it, I understand it will limit my ability to receive God's full blessings.

- Do everything in my power to bring God's purpose for my life to fruition *(faith without works is dead).*

- Don't take shortcuts; if I want to be true to my beliefs, then shortcuts do not exist.

- Remember on the down days to never give up on myself and the dreams God has given me.

I base every career decision, big and small, on these precepts. That's not an easy thing to do. There is a lot of temptation in every business from finance to academia to take the quick and easy path to success—to violate our values for promotion or because no one will ever know. I've felt pressure on numerous occasions to abandon my commitment to Christ, but then I remember the words of Jesus when he asked, "For what will it profit a man if he gains the whole world and loses his own soul?"

I can truly say there is nothing in this world worth giving up what I believe in.

I'm amazed at the number of people of all faiths I've met who don't understand that their faith is not an obstacle to fulfilling their dreams but the path *to* them. They don't understand the power that a total commitment to God grants them.

I spent a great deal of time not long ago with a young aspiring actor who talked about his career struggles: going to auditions, trying to get in to see casting directors, exhausting himself, not knowing what to do, going to church to try to hook up with this or that individual. I listened for a while and then said, "Where do you think God is in all of this? Have you prayed and looked for where he is leading you in your aspiration?"

He hadn't.

He was a Christian, but it never occurred to him that God had a place in his career pursuits.

I know from many of my own experiences that if you put your career in God's hands and trust him, you can't account for all the ways he will bless you. But you have to take that leap of faith, and even if you consider yourself a believer, that can be the hardest part. God's love is unconditional, but we need the faith to silence our own voice and listen to his. Then we can really hear what he's been trying to tell us about our careers all along.

I've written *Produced by Faith* to help you make that leap of faith. By sharing my story and my testimony of how my faith has actually been the greatest asset in my advancement, I hope to inspire you to take a new view of God's role in your career. At the end of the day, you don't have to choose between your faith and your work. Faith and works are two sides of the same coin.

PART ONE
DEVELOPMENT

CHAPTER ONE

YOU, THE MOVIE

*In the beginning
God created the heavens and the earth.*
—Genesis 1:1 NIV

The movie business is all about telling great stories. It's my job to identify those stories that will entertain audiences all over the world. Stories are built on setups and payoffs. When a screenwriter creates characters and situations in the first act of a film, those characters and situations have to pay off by the end. The bad guy goes to jail, the girl finally chooses the cool vampire instead of the hunky werewolf, and so on. If you don't have a payoff in the third act, you don't have a commercial movie . . . you have a bad student film.

I've found that one of the best ways to talk about how to

find success and keep your faith is by putting it in the context of your life as a story. It's much easier to put your trust in God when you can see your life and career as a story—with setups and payoffs, high points and low points just like every movie has.

The trouble is that when you are a character in a story—when you are immersed in it—you can't see how things will progress in the future. You lack perspective. It's tough to lose the job you loved, shrug, and say, "Oh well, God is obviously putting me in a position for something better to happen in a few weeks." It becomes very easy to assume that things will always be the way they are today. When things are going well, we sometimes lose perspective and start to think we're in control of things. But all it takes is one wrong turn and we quickly remember that's just not true.

The truth is, you and I are in control of only two things: how we *prepare* for what *might* happen and how we *respond* to what *just* happened. The moment when things actually *do* happen belongs to God.

You might be writing your story with the choices you make, but God is the director. Like all good directors, he has a vision for how your story will progress. He has a plan that will shape you into someone who can best serve him and this world. But how will you know what God has in mind for you unless you trust him to direct your story? Even when our faith seems to get in the way of our progress, we can remain faithful to God and trust his direction. That's been my approach since I got to Hollywood. It hasn't always been easy to remember that God has a plan for me, but whenever I have trusted in that plan and surrendered my fate to the Lord, he has done amazing things.

Another approach is to abandon God's path at the first sign of resistance and do whatever it takes to climb the ladder, regardless of cost. But before you do that, let me ask you this: What if you are just one bend in the road away from achieving your God-ordained purpose? If you give up on your faith now, could you live with knowing that your chance of a lifetime was only one act of faith away? I had a conversation recently with Will Smith about this idea; he told me that many people trying to make it get frustrated and don't give themselves over to the process of success. He said, "The distance between you and success isn't necessarily a yard—it's an inch. But to get that final inch is excruciating. You have to stay committed."

Then there's that word: *success*. It's a funny word with a lot of definitions. For some people, success means making a lot of money. Full stop. For others, it means fame. However, if you're really a Christian and you have made your faith the centerpiece of your life, then true success is much more than fortune or fame. Success is confidence and contentment in the person God has made you to be. Success is living a good, just, and honorable life, becoming the kind of person who inspires others to follow God. Success is also discovering and living in your purpose.

If you crave this kind of success in your career, then God's purpose must take the place of your own. Faith is your insurance. Even if you are laughed out of the conference room because of what you believe, your faith will reconcile what you lose and more than make up the difference in what you will gain. There are times when I get fearful or upset about something that doesn't work out in my favor, and in those moments, I have to remind myself that God is working. He will ultimately provide. He will help me get to my destination, even when it feels like I might be moving slower than I think I should or watching other people pass me by. The more we rely on God to direct our lives, the closer we draw to our ultimate purpose . . . even if we don't realize it.

THERE'S NOTHING ABOUT AMBITION that runs counter to Christianity. Joshua 1:8 also reads, "Keep this Book of the Law always on your lips; meditate on it day and night, so that you may be careful to do everything written in it. Then you will be prosperous and successful." When faith in God's purpose guides your feet on your career path, your work is blessed, because ultimately what you do serves God's higher purpose.

Career isn't everything. We have our families, our civic lives, and our private inner lives. But career permeates everything. You might spend half your adult life wanting to run a company, laboring to care for patients, teach students, defend the accused in court, sell homes, build homes, or write for newspapers—how can such a pursuit not shape who you become?

So if career is shaping who you become, and your faith isn't integrally involved in your career choices, then what good is your faith? It's time to start looking at your faith not as an obstacle to your career progress, but as an asset. A lot of times we don't look at faith in that way. But it's time to unify faith and career as dual assets toward achieving the same goal: our progress in becoming people who can have the maximum positive impact on this world. Career should be a spiritual pursuit, not just a physical or financial one. Your career should be where your dreams, aspirations, talents, and hopes for the present and future play out.

So how do we balance career and faith? How do we climb the ladder toward our vision of who we want to become while remaining true to the fundamentals that make us who we are? How do we serve God while operating in a realm that sometimes disrespects what we believe in, where we might be regarded as weird or irrational? How do we engage in, trust, and stay with the process when at times it looks as if we're going nowhere—or worse, going backward?

The key is remembering your story. The spiritual career journey parallels the steps involved in bringing a movie from the initial idea to theatrical release—a process known as Development and Production. In this process you are God's writing partner, God is the director, and each step is crucial. No idea becomes a movie without passing through these stages, and even though some of these stages can be difficult, tedious, or even painful, each leads to the next and hopefully to success.

Development is the often challenging, sometimes confounding process in which a raw idea slowly takes shape as a clear vision. In Hollywood, development starts when a writer or producer has an idea, something like "A disabled soldier goes native with an alien race and defends their beautiful civilization against his own people," which is the idea behind the blockbuster movie *Avatar.* In your career, Development begins when you have your first vision of what you want your future to look like. When you can see yourself as a lawyer, athlete, speaker, or engineer and decide to pursue a path that leads to the realization of that vision, Development is under way. It has its own distinct stages:

- WHAT'S THE BIG IDEA?—your vision for the kind of success you want to have and the person you want to become

- SELLING IT—when you find an employer or industry that will serve your goals and God's goals

- WRITING THE SCRIPT—making and following your plan through all its plot twists

- GETTING NOTES—when God gives you feedback and you (hopefully) listen and adjust your course

- DEVELOPMENT HELL—the times when you hit obstacles and must find a way past them

- GOD'S BUDGET AND PRODUCTION SCHEDULE—when you figure out what achieving your goals will cost and how long it will take

- IT'S ALL ABOUT CASTING—figuring out the people you need in your life to bring your story into production

- GOD'S GREEN LIGHT—when God brings you together with the opportunity you've been working toward

In Hollywood, a production executive oversees the development of a film, guiding the idea as it is shaped and refined. In your life, God should oversee the Development of your career. With a film idea, there are many points along the way where a project can fail and be abandoned. In your career pursuits, there are also many opportunities to surrender your principles or lose faith in God's direction. Through stories from my own career and the careers of others, I'm going to show you how important it is that you trust God and trust the process. If you stay true to your ideals, pay attention to the things God reveals to you, work hard, and surround yourself with good people, you will develop. You will grow in faith, wisdom, and ability—and eventually you will reach your goals.

When that happens, you go into Production. The stages of Production:

- *LIGHTS, CAMERA, ACTION!*—where you are in the position you've sought and now must perform and produce results for God

- *CUTTING IT TOGETHER*—where you experience how God will put the pieces of your career and faith together to create your road to success

- *MARKETING AND PUBLICITY*—in which God will market and promote who you are becoming

- *GOD'S DISTRIBUTION PLAN*—you see how the person God has shaped you to be impacts the larger world

- *YOU, THE SEQUEL* — God gets you ready for the next stage of your career

Production begins when God has fully shaped your vision, character, and talents and is ready to put you to work for his purpose. For a film, "going into production" signifies that it is time to turn the idea into a product. For you, Production occurs when you reach the position or career to which you have long aspired and you're ready to start really making things happen. You'll begin becoming someone who can have a meaningful impact on God's behalf. God will distribute your influence to the world and you and he will observe what kind of positive effect you can have on those around you. You'll reap some rewards and learn how you can improve the outcome the next time you're in Development.

In his wisdom, the Lord sends us on an endless, cyclical journey. That's what You, the Sequel, is all about. You'll achieve one goal for him, and immediately start working on another. He might send you back into Development again so that you can learn new lessons, test your faith, and grow wiser and stronger. He might even direct you into a new career. The more you trust God to lead you to glory, even through layoffs and setbacks, conflicts and failed ideas, the more success and joy you will find.

Through this book, my intent is to be your guide through all the stages of Development and Production, even as I move through those stages myself with no idea of what is coming tomorrow but infinite faith that God has a great plan. Along the way, I'll pass along some crucial strategies that I've learned about in my career, including:

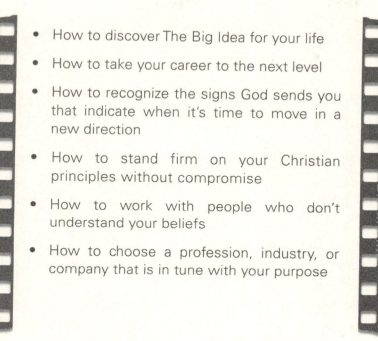

- How to discover The Big Idea for your life

- How to take your career to the next level

- How to recognize the signs God sends you that indicate when it's time to move in a new direction

- How to stand firm on your Christian principles without compromise

- How to work with people who don't understand your beliefs

- How to choose a profession, industry, or company that is in tune with your purpose

If I can take my personal ambition and my service to Christ and make both more successful without compromising, you can. Let this be your handbook for progressing in your career and your faith at the same time, without compromising either one.

CHAPTER TWO

WHAT'S THE BIG IDEA?

Where there is no vision, the people perish.
—Proverbs 29:18 KJV

We live in a world obsessed with instant success. You-Tube and reality television have rebooted the idea of success so that it's become unrecognizable. I landed my first internship in the film industry back in 1996, while I was still a freshman business major at the University of Southern California, and in just those few years since that time, things have changed so much I can hardly believe it. Today a poisonous idea persists that you can become famous overnight. In this line of thinking, fame = success. We have become impatient with the process, because we see fame as an end in itself. We tell ourselves that we can upload a wacky viral video to the

Internet or shock the world like Susan Boyle on *Britain's Got Talent* and bam! We have a three-book deal, we're sitting across the desk from David Letterman, and life is perfect. We think we can graduate from college and be CEO by the time we're thirty. In fact, more and more we think we're *entitled* to that. But it's a seductive mirage that is very dangerous.

There are no overnight successes. Everything comes with a cost.

Until the past ten years or so, most actors, writers, and directors followed the same basic career track: learn your craft, work as much as you possibly can, pay your dues, make contacts, and try to be in the right place at the right time when the Big Opportunity comes knocking.

It wasn't easy, and it wasn't supposed to be. The difficulty of sticking to a plan that could take twenty years to pay off meant that for the most part the people who finally "made it" possessed the commitment, dedication, and skill set necessary to have long-lasting, high-quality careers. It's kind of like the rigorous training that world-class athletes of any sport endure—by the time you've gone through the work and struggle to become a champion, you've also developed the wisdom and discipline to sustain that level of performance.

Overnight celebrity culture undercuts the process of change that we all must undergo in order to achieve the true success that I've talked about.

I'm not going to reiterate the usual talk about persistence and passion and work ethic; you already know how important it is to develop those qualities if you're going to have a life of health, joy, prosperity, and service to God. Instead, ask yourself this: What if you actually land the dream position *and you're not ready for it?*

Let's role-play for a minute. You bust out of school convinced of your own genius, work Facebook and LinkedIn like a master, make all the right contacts, and before you know it at age twenty-five you've got the ideal job you've always wanted. You've arrived.

But are you really *ready*? See, while your career was in the fast lane, your character was still in the slow lane. While you were playing the game and shaking hands and working the Internet, you didn't become the person you needed to be in order to make the most of this opportunity. You don't know how to manage people, make decisions, or resolve conflicts. You've muscled your way to the top, but now that you're in your dream job, there are no excuses for poor performance—and you don't have the tools to do the job at the level it requires. But you're desperate to keep it, by any means necessary, even if it means betraying every principle and ideal you possess. In the end, you might survive, but it'll cost you more than you ever thought. More likely, you'll betray your own ethics, betray people you care about, fail in the end, and possibly ruin your chances for success in your chosen field for the rest of your life.

When you get something that you don't work for, you won't know how to value or maintain it.

When we can't find something inherent in our character or abilities that validates the position we've attained, we become insecure, and that deep-seated insecurity will eat us alive. God allows us to struggle and work through setbacks for a simple reason: he wants us to grow and develop the character and competency that ultimately enable us to succeed on our own merits. When we trust the plan and invest the time in our own Development, we'll be ready when the long-sought position finally appears. When we don't, our dream job can become a nightmare.

God wants you to go through Development before you go into Production. No studio would green-light a movie that hadn't gone through a rigorous development process (and those that do get green-lit quickly are the exception, not the rule). Production would be a money-losing disaster.

That's what happens when you try to bypass God's plan for your personal Development and try to go right into Production. You might land the gig, but odds are you won't be ready for the responsibility and will be consumed by it. If you don't like the idea of starting in the mail room and working your way up the ladder for fifteen years, how would you feel about being finished in your chosen profession as quickly as you got started? And as you will see in these pages, I thank God that I didn't get the things I was praying for early in my career because if I had, I would have burned out long ago.

You must pass through each stage of Development before you're ready for Production. There are no shortcuts, not if you want to achieve success. Even Jesus had to get through Development. He didn't begin his ministry until he was thirty years old, and it lasted only three years. It took thirty years of Development to produce just three years of Production. For thirty years he developed his skill set and his ability to understand and relate to the people he would ultimately deliver. He learned how to be a leader from the ground up. Everyone must go through Development.

*   *   *

IT'S ALL ABOUT THE Big Idea. In Hollywood every movie starts this way. The idea might come from an existing property like a book, comic book, or television show, or it might be an original pitch developed by a writer, producer, or director. In any case, someone from a production company comes to a studio like Columbia and pitches an idea to someone like me. The pitch might take the form of a completed screenplay (called a "spec script"), a film treatment (a detailed narrative version of the film's story), or a verbal pitch where the writer or producer describes the idea, existing movies that it's similar to, and maybe some name actors who might be attached to it. If I like the concept and it has commercial viability—and if the person pitching has a good track record—then I will take the project to my bosses and advocate that it is worth pursuing.

If they like it, then we'll buy the idea and now it becomes part of our development slate. We'll "option" the idea, meaning that we have the exclusive right to develop it for a certain period. Sometimes, a studio will keep a project in development for years while the script is reworked and the idea is refined. It's the job of someone like me to find ideas that can become movies, then to shepherd them to the point where they can actually go into production. My job performance is judged largely on the films I develop and the ones I oversee in production each year.

For you the Development process is similar. You begin it by declaring your Big Idea and asking questions about who you want to become in your career and life:

- What are you passionate about?

- What are you naturally good at doing?

- What kind of things are you interested in?

- What kind of family life, marriage, lifestyle, and church life do you envision for yourself?

- What do you believe God wants you to achieve for him in your career?

- What do you feel called by God to do?

In the end, the last question is the most important, because if you make your career choices according to the call God has on your life, he will open doors for you that you cannot possibly predict.

The path to Production begins with the discovery of the Big Idea of your life. But how do we discover that idea? God doesn't always send you a vision in picture perfect HD— sometimes it's more like watching one of those old home movies shot in grainy 8mm. We have to squint to see what's going on and we miss so much detail that sometimes we lose the story completely.

However, God sometimes intends for us to gain insight from the clues provided to us through the circumstances of our lives. That's what happened to me: the tragedy and challenge of my early days shaped who I have become and the path I walk every single day.

I DIDN'T HAVE THE constant positive presence of a father growing up. My father, Donald Ray, and my mother, Paulette, met when they were teenagers and it was love at first sight. They got married young and lived in Oakland, California. My dad was an attractive, charismatic guy, the life of the party, always very good with people and very good in business. He and my mom had their first child, my brother Donald Ray II, when they were in their early twenties. They moved to the suburbs and my dad went to work for UPS. I was born about three years later. Life was good.

Dad started moving up within UPS very fast. He was good at what he did, and he had a great personality—the gift of gab. In a few years, he quickly rose from delivery person to supervisor. He was climbing the corporate ladder, but the social aspects of the job started taking their toll. He would go out after work a lot and drink as a way to fit in with his colleagues and superiors. This is nothing new; our jobs are as much social as they are professional. However, the problem with my dad was that his father was an alcoholic, as were two of his brothers; the warning signs were there. But with the pressures of work and the desires driven by his ambition, he ignored the signs and his drinking began to get out of control.

He started missing work. My mother took a receptionist's job because Dad was becoming more unreliable, going in and out of the house, sometimes disappearing for the day just to go and drink. Once, when I was very young, he came home drunk and had my mom pinned to the bed. He never hit her, he just kept yelling at her. I remember standing in the corner, on the other side of the room, terrified.

You can probably fill in some of the rest; this isn't an unusual story. My younger brother, David, was born when I was close to four years old. Shortly after that we lost the house because my father lost his job and stopped paying the bills, and Mom wasn't making enough to cover the mortgage.

Then one day, Dad left.

My mom took us three boys and moved us into my grandparents' two-bedroom, one-bath, 1,000-square-foot house in Richmond, California. Imagine the blow: a dynamic woman living the American dream, forced to move back in with her parents! But like so many women before her, she did what she had to do to take care of her children. Pops and Goggi had a motor home and they slept there at night so we could have their bedroom. Everyone sacrificed.

More proof that pride goeth before a fall: Mom applied for welfare. I spent a good deal of my childhood living on food stamps. I didn't understand it, but when one of my friends at school teased me about it, I yelled "I am *not* on welfare!" and ran home to ask my grandmother. She just nodded and quietly broke the news to me with as much dignity as she could muster: "Yes, your mom does get assistance from the government to help take care of you all." I remember being terribly upset. Surely there had to be a reason all this was happening to us.

Slowly, things improved and stabilized. After a couple of years, Mom got a job at a day care center and we moved into an apartment. She began going to school to earn her degree in child care and development. My father still came around once in a while; we learned he had had a few unsuccessful stints in rehab. Unfortunately he was usually drunk and not the loving man we had sometimes known him to be. On one occasion, when my little brother was four or five, Mom let my dad stay at the house for the night. He kept asking her for the keys to our car, but she refused, knowing that he would end up driving drunk and possibly hurting himself and God knew who else. Finally, my baby brother, not knowing any better, went into her purse and gave him the keys. The next morning the car was gone; later that day, Dad showed up with my uncle, both so drunk they could barely stand. I got to school late that day, frustrated and angry about all that was happening to my family.

What still amazes me about those days is that Mom never spoke negatively about my father. She must have known that he was in the grip of a disease and that this wasn't who he really was. Because of that, I never looked at him as less than a man. He was still my father.

He disappeared again for a long time. We didn't know where he was, and life kept going on. When I was nine, he resurfaced; he had stopped smoking and drinking and was living in Oakland in a tiny apartment behind the restaurant where he worked. He came around and he and my mother spent a lot of time talking and trying to repair the wounds of the past. He was very apologetic and humble, and desperately wanted to work his way back into our lives. Slowly, Mom let him come around more often, and we would go to eat at his restaurant. Everything was looking up until one Sunday night we got a call: Dad had suffered a heart attack.

He had experienced heart problems before (we later found out that he needed a heart transplant but had kept it secret) and when we saw him in the hospital it seemed like the attack was minor, because he was up talking and feeling great. He was telling us how he was going to start coming with us to church and how we were going to be a family again. The next day, we got home after school and were getting ready to visit him again in the hospital. I was on the couch reading *Where the Sidewalk Ends* by Shel Silverstein and the phone rang.

The next thing I remember was my mom screaming, "No! No! No!" over and over. Dad had another massive heart attack, and this one took him down. Dead at age thirty-six. My mom was a wreck. She could barely drive, so we picked up my Aunt Sondra and rushed to the hospital. My mom walked my brothers and me into the hospital room where his body lay. She told us gently, "Kiss your father good-bye."

I kissed him on the forehead. I still remember how cold he was.

It was February of 1988.

I didn't want to go to the funeral; they made me go. But I left early. I didn't know how to deal with this. Why would God take my father from me just as he was getting his life together? It didn't make sense. Even now, I wrestle with it.

My mother was a real-life superhero in raising three boys, and she ended up buying the day care center where she worked. But a boy needs a father. Only a man can teach a boy how to be a man. Boys who don't have their fathers can suffer from a wide range of problems. They become troubled, or become overachievers to compensate, or many variations in between. I became an overachiever, but that was my mechanism for coping with pain I had no idea how to process. I became closed off and harbored a lot of anger and anxiety. To see your father alive one day, and the next day he's laid out in the morgue, and you don't get to say good-bye—no words can describe this type of hurt. It was a difficult experience that made me extremely self-reliant, and not necessarily in a good way. Even today, I struggle with the fallout of my fatherlessness.

I'm a middle child, and middle children tend to become rebels. I became a rebel in reverse. I started trying to do everything and help everyone. Around this time, my uncle started a church in Oakland called Wings of Love Maranatha Ministries, which I'll talk more about later. I became part of that church, and it gave me the outlet that I needed. I was on the student council at school, but involvement at Wings of Love gave me a purpose. I just wanted to be involved and somehow make a contribution that would help make everything better.

Entertainment also became an outlet. A few years earlier, I remember seeing *Rocky III* and falling in love with the "against all odds" sports drama. Another film, *The Color Purple*, had a profound impact on me. I also became a huge fan of *The Cosby Show*; I would tune in religiously every week. After my dad died, it gave me tremendous hope because no matter what challenge the Huxtables faced, they would always get through it as a family. My mom couldn't afford to send me or my brothers to counseling to help us deal with all we had been through, so going to church and watching movies and TV became my therapy.

I understood the inner workings of the church, but film and TV were a mystery. Who made all this happen? Who wrote the script? Who paid the actors? I became obsessed with learning everything I could about the entertainment industry (movies in particular) and how it worked.

When I became a freshman in high school, I was still holding on to a childhood dream of becoming a running back for the Dallas Cowboys. I used to dream of running across the field and scoring touchdowns like Cowboy greats

Tony Dorsett and Herschel Walker. Was that where the Lord was leading me?

At my first scrimmage during football tryouts, I got knocked unconscious.

Message received loud and clear, Lord . . . Hollywood it is.

That was my Big Idea, to pursue a career in the entertainment industry.

SO HOW DO YOU find your Big Idea? Here are three fundamental questions you should ask yourself:

- How have the events of your past (both good and bad) given you clues to help you discover what God really wants you to do with your life?

- What gifts and talents has he blessed you with? What do you do best?

- When you close your eyes and imagine, what vision of your life brings you the most peace?

While you are considering the Big Idea for your future, consider this: It's got to be about more than getting promoted, getting a raise, or even becoming a star. It must also be about how you can make an impact on the world and become a living example of God's divine power.

When I think of how I discovered the Big Idea for my life,

there is no question that my father's death was a major factor. It made me determined to make something of my life and to fulfill the potential in myself that was cut short in him. Remember that God has strategically allowed every moment in your story to play out in order to help prepare you for your purpose.

IF YOU ARE STRUGGLING with figuring out your Idea, this is invaluable: Identify people in your current or desired profession who are doing what you think you should do. Contact them. Talking to others who have found success doing what you are considering will help you fine-tune your Big Idea. Even if you already know your Idea, it is still invaluable to sit down with as many leaders in your industry as possible.

At USC, while I was still honing my Big Idea, I met with as many people as I could, including the legendary Quincy Jones, David Gale (former president of MTV Films), and Damon Lee (former senior vice president of MGM). I gained invaluable insight about the business and this knowledge gave me even more confidence that I was pursuing the right path. If you can find people who have reached the top of the mountain while being open about their faith, find out how they did it. Ask challenging questions about how they stayed strong and how they dealt with criticism or peer pressure. Just as important, find out how they benefited from staying true to their principles. You may be quite surprised to learn how many unique opportunities come to those who do not follow the herd and whose motives can be trusted by those at the highest levels.

There are many, many examples. In professional sports you can find many athletes who openly and proudly profess their Christian faith and live according to its principles, including former Super Bowl MVP quarterback Kurt Warner, ex-Laker A. C. Green, and Cy Young Award–winning pitcher Orel Hershiser. In entertainment, people such as singer Amy Grant, actor Angela Bassett, and actor Neal McDonough are just a few of the successful Christians.

Use the examples of others to help you see God's vision for your life more clearly. If you do, you'll set better goals, identify specific skills you need to acquire, and have a more realistic picture of what it will take to get your Big Idea into production. For me, making successful films is the means to an end: using great characters and stories to communicate to millions the benefit that comes from living with character, compassion, courage, and love. Ultimately, my career vision is to use film as a way to inspire and bring people hope. When you have the goals, skills, and purpose clearly in mind, you're ready to sell your story.

- How will your goal serve God in the long term?

- Are you out to be the best in your line of work?

- If not, why are you there?

- How prepared are you to lose a job for your Christian values?

- What values and beliefs are not subject to compromise?

- If you will compromise on some, why?

- What kind of impact do you want to have on your chosen profession?

WiMO ENABLED

CHAPTER THREE

SELLING IT

Character may be called the most
effective means of persuasion.
—Aristotle, *Rhetoric*, Book Two

I doubt that when Matthew wrote the words "When you pray, enter into your closet," he had a men's bathroom stall in mind, but that's where I was. There was no other quiet place in the office. And I desperately needed a moment alone to deal with the crisis I was in. The stall was cold from the air-conditioning, my feet were firmly placed on the beige concrete tile, and my head was in my hands. There was nobody else in the bathroom but me. It was totally silent except for the intense conversation that I was having with God. I was crying out to him—sure, I was doing it under my breath, but I was shouting from the bottom of my soul.

"Lord, help me," I said. "I believe in your Word, and you said that if I knocked, you would answer. You said that anything I asked for in the name of Jesus you would grant. Well, I need you to do something on this job today, Lord. If what you say is true, God, if your *Word* is true, then I need you to move in this situation today." And that was it. I'd left my cosmic voice mail. I stood up, brushed the wrinkles out of my pants, washed my hands out of habit, and went back to my frustrating job.

Most of us have experienced at least one such moment of sheer desperation—a true dark night of the soul. We want what we want *now* and we can't understand why God isn't answering. In poker terms, it's an "all in" moment when you have the audacity to call God out and say, "Prove it, Lord." Faith is the substance of things hoped for and the evidence of things unseen; getting to that desperation place often means our faith is wavering because we haven't seen that for which our spirit cries out. Maybe you gave God your ultimatum over a relationship or a crisis of faith. For me, it was about a dream that seemed to be deferred and dying.

It was 2002, I was 23 years old, six years after I'd landed my first internship with Handprint Entertainment in 1996, four years after I had joined Overbrook Entertainment as an intern, and close to two years after my graduation from USC. As I mentioned, I had big aspirations to work in Hollywood. In the beginning I was an intern, which was all right. I was learning the business and getting a chance to know Will Smith and James Lassiter (JL), who started the company and became (and still are) great mentors and friends.

When I graduated in 2000, I stopped being an intern and became James Lassiter's second assistant. That doesn't sound glamorous, but I wasn't just getting coffee. I was doing a lot of the things that executives typically did, from attending development meetings to reading scripts. Life was fun and interesting. I was twenty-two, single, and living in L.A., earning pretty good money, and I expected that in a year or so I would get the chance to move up to the junior executive position that I coveted.

Then 2000 became 2001. Nothing happened. Will's movie *Ali* came out and Will got his first Academy Award nomination, which I figured would lead to more opportunity at Overbrook and more projects. That might mean a need for new executive talent, and I knew I was ready. So I waited . . .

And still nothing happened.

You might be thinking that I was expecting a lot. After all, I was a kid only a year out of school, but I had put in my time. Instead of going home to Oakland and my family, I had interned every year and summer while at USC. Two of those four years I interned at Overbrook, so Will and JL knew what I could do. It wasn't out of line for me to expect to hit the fast lane in a year.

Only I wasn't even on the road.

I was on the shoulder waving traffic flares with smoke coming from under my hood.

I was beginning to realize that the opportunity I had hoped for might never come. I knew that Will and JL liked me and thought I had talent; it wasn't a matter of them passing me by. But the hardest leap in Hollywood is the leap from assistant to executive. When you're an executive, it's usually easier to move up because you have the opportunity to prove you can do the work and get movies made. But when you're an assistant, you feel like the only thing the rest of the world thinks you're good for is managing "no cream, two sugars." It's that way in most industries, especially when there is so much money and reputation on the line.

By the fall of 2001, I was frustrated and depressed. You ever felt like that, when work knocks you flat? Assistant work can be mundane; I felt as if I was stuck on a treadmill. I did my own cost-benefit analysis of my experience, and the cost of being an assistant was definitely outweighing the benefit. It got to the point where I didn't even want to come into the office. From my perspective, I didn't matter; my contributions to the company felt like they meant nothing. The most important thing to me has always been that my contributions are valued, that my work makes things better for others, and that people need what I can do.

I wasn't getting that sense on any level. I was just showing up, and nobody wants "just showed up" on their headstone. I hadn't gone home during summers. One summer I worked at the dean's office of the USC film school, the Gap, and kept my internship just to scrape together enough money to support myself. I had gone "all in" on my dream. For nothing? I was praying on the question, but not getting any guidance from God on what I should do.

Finally, in early 2002, I couldn't take it anymore. I was miserable. I was sitting in my cubicle feeling empty and down and trapped and I said, *"I've got to do something."* That's how I ended up in the bathroom stall, dropping an ultimatum on God. It was time for him to make a move. That was the day that literally changed my life and opened my eyes.

*   *   *

EVEN WHEN YOU HAVE discovered the Big Idea for your career, you're not in Development yet. In the career realm, there's another key player without which your story can't be told: your employer. This is the organization that takes a risk on you and gives you a venue in which you can make mistakes, learn, test yourself, and slowly master your profession. If your career is where you develop the character, talents, and influence to achieve God's will, your employer (or in some cases, your mentor or university) provides the opportunity for you to do so.

In the movie business, before an idea can go into Development it has to be sold. When a writer or producer has a book to adapt or a great idea for a movie, he or she will come into our offices and pitch it to us. In the current industry climate, it is becoming more difficult to sell material, so many producers now will include in their pitch facts about the target audience demographics, the box office performance of similar films, marketable actors and directors already interested in the film, a possible budget range, and anything else that might help us decide that this Big Idea is worth the risk of inserting into the Development pipeline.

You have to sell your vision to an employer. This will allow you to begin your career and "flip the switch" on the Development process. This will usually mean doing interviews where you are expected not only to communicate your qualifications but to share your ideas on how you can become a person of value to the company. I have undergone this process several times already in my career, from interviews for my first internships all the way to my first executive job at MGM.

So let me pass on the wisdom that will probably make the

difference between success and failure as you start knocking on doors and sorting through your best interview clothes: *Do your homework.* Once you have your company list, do as much research as you can about each one. Find out about their history, philosophy, marketing, distribution, track record, and so on. But most important, what kinds of products does the company make? If you were to become employed by that company, what would those products say about your faith?

If you do this, you'll know who you're suited for. If you pay attention to which studios release what types of movies, you'll start to notice a pattern. Some studios release only family- or teen-oriented pictures with a rating of PG-13 or lower. Others mostly release more intense PG-13 films or R-rated films. Some studios never do horror or heavy violence whereas others specialize in it. Each company has its niche, and a smart producer would never pitch a studio on a film that's out of its niche. For example, you would never pitch the R-rated horror series *Saw* to Disney. Can you imagine: Walt Disney presents *Saw*? It would never happen because that's not the type of movie they make, and the market doesn't want those types of movies from them.

When you're looking for the right companies to try to sell on your pitch, know which ones are a good fit for who you are and what you want. I can't stress this enough. So many times we just want to get a job—any job—and we never ask ourselves, "What kind of company do I want to work for?" Or "Where does God want me to be employed?" Ask yourself these questions, and then as best you can, start identifying companies you feel are the best fit for building the career you desire.

Pretty regularly, someone will ask me for advice about a career in Hollywood, and I'll ask them, "What preparation have you done?" All too often, the answer is a shrug. I've been there when people come in to interview and they are not knowledgeable about the company. It's an instant indication that they are not really serious about getting the job, and it reflects a lack of overall passion about their career aspirations. There is too much competition for too few jobs (especially in film), and if you haven't prepared, your Big Idea may never sell.

I DON'T KNOW WHAT I was expecting following my fervent bathroom prayer, but God moved so fast it almost scared me. Usually, I wouldn't leave the office until JL left. Well, at the end of that day, about 7 p.m., he and I were the only ones left in the office. In almost four years, JL and I had *never* been the last two people left in the office. There were always other people around. But not that night.

After a while, he came over to my desk and said, "DeVon, you got a minute?"

Hmm. Sounded ominous. I followed JL into his office and we sat down. "DeVon," he said, "Will and I really like you and you do great work, and we know that you have hit a wall here. We're not set up for the kind of growth that you need. Because of that, we're going to help you find a new job."

Wow. It took me a second to gather my thoughts, and then I said, "Okay, cool. What's our time line?" JL said that we didn't have a time line for now. He told me that if I made a list of industry people I knew and others I thought might be hiring, he would make as many calls as I needed. I was humbled that he could see the potential in me and incredibly grateful for his generous offer to help. I walked out thinking about my list and my future.

Outside the office, several things hit me squarely between the eyes. One, I was blown away that God had heard me. I had asked him to move on my job situation that day, and he had. He'd heard me and made something happen. I felt exalted and humbled.

Have you ever experienced a moment when you knew God has just put his hand on your life? If you have, then you know it's unforgettable. No matter how deep your faith, seeing God intervene directly and transparently in your life sends a chill up the spine.

Then came the other realization . . . I had to start looking for a new job.

I made a list of everyone I knew in the business. Then I looked for available junior executive jobs. But nothing shook loose. After six or eight weeks, JL asked me how the search was going. "Slowly," I said. I told him I was out there pounding the pavement but there were no jobs. He told me to keep him posted and that he'd continue to make calls, too, but there wasn't much to keep him posted about. I had to make something happen. But I was wondering why God would start something and leave it up to me to finish on my own.

I left a message for Will with his assistant, and later that day he came over to my cubicle. I told him my situation and asked him if he could set up a meeting with Richard Lovett and Ken Stovitz at Creative Artists Agency (CAA) about them helping me get a job. CAA is one of the most powerful talent agencies in Hollywood. If they made a few calls, I would have a job. I was sure of it.

Will has one of the biggest hearts of anyone I know, and he came through like the champ that he is. I had a great meeting with Richard and Ken. The only thing they said disappointed them was that I didn't want to be an agent. They told me they'd hire me on the spot if I wanted to work for them. That wasn't what I wanted. But they were kind enough to offer to make some calls on my behalf and turn over a few rocks to make something happen. I left that meeting feeling good about my prospects.

You can predict the result. Zero. But it wasn't because they didn't follow through on their word. Richard and Ken got numerous meetings for me and I had some great interviews, but nothing panned out. I asked myself, "What is going on?" I was confused. How is that I had such tremendous support yet still no job? I was doing my best to stay faithful but truthfully . . . I was starting to stress. We were coming up on Easter and I was still stuck on the treadmill. Then I got a call out of the blue from Tracey Edmonds, who runs Edmonds Entertainment Group and has produced movies like *Soul Food* and *Josie and the Pussycats*. Her assistant said they had heard about my job search and wondered if I would be interested in meeting about a junior executive position they had open in the film division.

The next Friday, I was at the Edmonds Entertainment office, ready to impress. It turned out that an agent was encouraging Tracey to interview more senior people than me, but she persisted. I met with the two executives who were running the film division, the meeting went well, and

I walked away with the by-now-familiar refrain of "We'll call you and let you know what happens" ringing in my ears.

Of course, by this time I was afraid to get my hopes up. I was also a wreck. I was sleepwalking through my duties at Overbrook because I had one foot out the door, and I was scared that this lead, too, would be a dead end. Most of all, I was worried that God had placed his hand on my life to make something happen, and I wouldn't be able to close the deal. It was a miserable time.

Have you known times when you simply cannot fathom what God could be up to, what he wants from you, or what you're supposed to do next? When that happens, so often we try to figure out the next step for ourselves when we should stop, quiet our minds, and listen to God's voice speaking to us.

I found out that Bishop T.D. Jakes was in town speaking, so I went to hear him. He was preaching a message called "Turn the Page." He talked about how at the end of the book of Deuteronomy, Moses died. The Hebrews were in mourning, not knowing how they would go on. But, said Bishop Jakes, the story doesn't end there. When you turn the page to the book of Joshua, God tells the Israelites to get up and stop mourning, and he gives them Joshua to lead them into the Promised Land. The message was clear: If you simply stop moving forward because you are devastated by your past, then there is no hope. But if you simply turn the page from your old situation to a new one, your story will continue, and God already has a plan to lead you into the land he has promised.

This was like an electrical current for me. I took the

words of Bishop Jakes to mean that I had to turn the page and have faith that God had a plan for me. What if God had my destiny waiting to reveal itself at the appropriate time if I would just act on faith alone, even though I had no idea what my next job would be?

I quit my job. On Monday, I gave my two weeks' notice at Overbrook. People were shocked that I was walking away from a job when I didn't have to. Some asked, "Man, what are you doing?" I told them I believed that if I had faith and believed God was in control, then I had to do this. I had to walk by faith, not by sight. Faith without works is no good. I had no idea if the job with Tracey Edmonds was going to come to pass, but sometimes, the only way to reach a goal is to surrender to God.

You may have experienced this. Until that time, I hadn't. But I knew that I had given God an ultimatum in my bathroom prayer and he had come through. Maybe the reason I hadn't gotten my big break was that I wasn't fulfilling my end of the bargain. The Lord had put it all on the line for me, but what had I done? I'd gone on interviews. All I had left was to strip away every other means of support and place my fate (and faith) entirely in his hands.

Week One went by. Nothing. Overbrook hired someone to replace me, and I helped her get acclimated, which is like tying the rope around your own neck when you're standing on the gallows. I called Tracey's office and they said she was traveling. Nobody knew anything. The weekend after that first week, before the countdown to unemployment *really* got ticking, I had a man-to-man with God. "Lord," I said, "this can't be about a job. Your Word says the cattle on a thousand hills are yours. So what you want from me has to be more than just something physical or material. It must be spiritual. There's some way you want me to grow spiritually. So I must go after it spiritually."

On Monday I started fasting. I drank juices but ate no solid food. By Wednesday, nada. The Lord was going to make this tough. Fine, I said. I'm tough. I can take it. On Thursday, I drank nothing but water. I needed God to know that I was going to leave it all on the court. I was going to do anything that I had to in order to prove to him that I was serious.

But at the same time, my larger prayer took on a new emphasis. I stopped just praying about a job. Instead, I asked the Lord that if entertainment was not a door that he was going to open, would he please reveal that to me. "Not my will but thine be done," I said many times. If being in the film business was not the path he had in mind, I trusted that he would keep the doors shut. If that happened, I had no choice but to suck it up and accept the fact that the Lord had other plans for me, whether I was crazy about them or not.

I think that was the pivotal moment, my tipping point. We all struggle with ego and a sense of entitlement. We think we're smart enough to know how to navigate through this complicated life, or that what we want is what is best for us. In reality, we don't have the answers. God does. In the past, when you stopped trying to force the action and let God take the wheel, didn't wonderful, unexpected things come to pass? This wasn't a question of where I was going to work or even what industry I was going to be in. It was about who I was going to be in God's eyes—his servant or my own.

I made the decision to let him know I was his.

Friday, I was faint and light-headed from hunger when I went to work. This was a problem. There was going to be a going-away lunch in my honor, and I didn't want to pass out. So I said, "Lord, I have done all I can, the rest is in your hands," and I ate. I went to work, went to the party, said a few words, then at the end of the day gathered my things into a box and left . . . without a job.

Monday morning broke as the first day of unemployment in my life. It was surreal. I didn't know where to go or what to do with myself. I can understand the devastating effect that being unemployed has on people, especially when they've been out of work for a long time. We are what we do. We need purpose in our lives, and having a job provides some of that purpose. What was my purpose now? What was I supposed to do?

Later, my mom called in a panic. I hadn't told anybody what I was doing because I didn't want to have the same "DeVon, are you nuts?" conversation fifty times. Mom had called Overbrook to talk to me and been informed that I no longer worked there. She asked me how I was going to earn a living and pay my rent. I didn't have any good answers to those questions, so I just told her that I would handle things, apologized for making her worry, and promised to call her later.

At about five o'clock that afternoon, as I was getting a full sense of how depressing daytime talk shows are, my phone rang. It was from Edmonds Entertainment, calling to offer me the junior executive job at Edmonds. "Do you still want it?" they asked.

I played it cool. I put them on hold so I could do a little

holy dance and shout. Then I got back on the line and said, "Yes!" One week later, I started my first job as an executive in the movie business. I was in Development, with the new-found understanding that while Hollywood is an industry built on relationships, my most treasured relationship should always be the one I have with God. For if I seek him first, there is no door in his will for my life that he will not open.

ONE OF THE LESSONS of my Overbrook story—apart from "never keep secrets from your mother"—is that doing your research and having a skill set is only part of the selling process. The other essential part is to understand that his Word is true. Proverbs 3:5–6 says, "Trust in the Lord with all your heart; do not depend on your own understanding. Seek his will in all you do, and he will show you which path to take" (NLT). Quitting my job and then fasting were my way of showing him, "I'm putting everything in your hands."

Finding a job is as much a spiritual endeavor as it is a physical one. I'm thankful that early in my career God put me through this process so I could learn this valuable lesson: *Actions speak louder than words.* I could say that I wanted his will in my life and pray that he would give me a job, but what more was I willing to do to unlock my spiritual destiny? How hard was I willing to fight for it spiritually? Was I willing to put it all on the line and trust that he would provide?

As you look for places to sell your Big Idea, ask yourself this: "Am I ready to show God and this prospective employer that I mean what I say?" Spiritually, that means you must diligently seek God's will in your job search through prayer, fasting, and personal sacrifice. Challenge yourself to go deeper than you ever have spiritually as a means to display to God how serious you are to have his will operate in your life. Practically, that might mean working as an intern, taking a position below what you think you're qualified for, accepting a probationary period of employment, or working on a temporary project-to-project basis. If the job fits your vision, you do what you must to prove that you and only you possess the talent, drive, and ethical fitness to become an invaluable asset.

Selling yourself to an employer while remaining true to your identity as a Christian seems difficult but is actually easier than you might think. It's really a matter of following some simple steps:

Step One: Believe that it is possible. You must believe that God has a plan for your career where your faith and your professional responsibilities can coexist. You have to believe in your soul that you can be both a successful, ambitious professional and a committed follower of Christ.

Step Two: Know the point of your story. Interviewers wade through hundreds of résumés and dozens of interviewees in order to find someone extraordinary. Companies want people with a vision both for how they can grow and how their growth can make the organization stronger. Be that person. Have precise goals in mind: You want to develop a new software product, be a newspaper's first female foreign corre-spondent, or open up a new sales territory. Remember, your life is a story. Tell it.

Step Three: Don't be afraid to come clean. In the Sermon on the Mount, Jesus tells his listeners not to "hide their light under a bushel." Meaning, don't hide who you truly are. There was a time when I wasn't sure my Sabbath commitment and my work in enter-tainment were compatible. But I made a critical deci-sion in my first internship interview that helped me resolve this issue forever. Before I accepted the job, I nervously told the office manager that I didn't work on the Sabbath and if working on the Sabbath was a condition of the job then I would have to decline the internship. To my surprise and delight, she said, "No problem." This moment gave me tremendous confi-dence that I could be who I was and still find suc-cess in this business. In every interview since I haven't hesitated to be vocal about my commitment and it's never been an issue. Don't be afraid to express to a potential employer any "spiritual deal breakers" you may have. Trust and know that if it's the job God has for you, it will all work out.

Step Four: Let your actions preach for you. The greatest testament of your faith is your day-to-day conduct. Once you've stated your faith, let that be that. Talk is cheap, especially in a job interview. Your actions will tell your superiors and coworkers just how Christian you are or aren't. One of the unfortunate truths in today's society is that Christianity is having a PR crisis. Many people who publicly claim to be Christians have done damage to Christianity by displaying behavior that's anything but: adultery, corruption, etc. It's unfortunate, because the actions of a few impact the perception of many. So it's even more important to let your actions speak for you. If you are true to your faith in goodwill, honesty, fidelity, and trustworthiness, it will be apparent in everything you do.

Step Five: Don't be afraid to walk away. No position is worth compromising your beliefs. It is not enough to have faith; works have to follow. If you interview with an employer and it's evident the job is not a good fit for your faith, don't accept it. It's much better to have peace of mind knowing God still has the right job out there for you instead of accepting one out of fear that you know isn't right. There will be other, better opportunities.

This concept of selling yourself to God may seem strange, but there's actually a precedent: Daniel, Shadrach, Meshach, and Abednego did it. They had to show God they were willing to lose their very lives if it meant doing something on the job that wouldn't be pleasing to him. Proving not only our sincerity but our total willingness to be his servants as we pursue our career is critical. Though I didn't really know it at the time, that is what I was doing when I quit my Overbrook job and began fasting. I was showing God that I wasn't afraid to let go of the wheel and put him in charge. I showed him that I trusted his plan for me enough to get out of the way and let it unfold.

That's not an easy thing to do. We're accustomed to feeling like the masters of the universe; it's uncomfortable for us not to try to control every aspect of our lives. But trusting and loving God can't just be things we say; if they are, they become no more sincere than the words on a Hallmark card. God expects us to put our money where our faith is in all aspects of life, especially career. I think that's why I got the call from Edmonds Entertainment after I finally told the Lord that if he didn't want me to be in movies, that was fine with me. I was 100 percent sincere in my desire to serve him in whatever way he chose, and he knew it. When I became his instrument spiritually as well as physically, I was ready for the door to my career to be unlocked and my Development progressed.

If signs in your life point you to a position that is nothing like the one you had in mind, perhaps God foresees that you will do great good there. Will you accept, or impose your will over his? The tests never end, but if you put your faith first, neither do the rewards.

When you have sold yourself successfully to a company and to God, you will enter Development, on the way to God's green light.

- How much have you researched the companies you would like to join?

- How do your personal values and moral code make you an asset to an employer?

- Have you already received signs from God regarding your career direction?

- Have you heeded those signs? If not, why not?

- What are you doing to show God that you have faith in his plan for your future?

CHAPTER FOUR

WRITING THE SCRIPT

The tablets were the work of God;
the writing was the writing of God,
engraved on the tablets.
—Exodus 32:16 NIV

In 1990, screenwriter Tom Schulman won the Academy Award for Best Original Screenplay for *Dead Poets Society*, but when he went to the press room with presenter Jane Fonda to answer questions from the members of the press, he was reminded of the writer's traditional place in the Hollywood pecking order. The press corps plied Ms. Fonda with questions about her newly minted relationship with mogul Ted Turner, and after she insisted that the night belonged to Schulman, a reporter turned to the writer and said, "Do you think she'll marry Ted?" Rim shot. Blackout.

Unfortunately, that is how a lot of writers can be treated in the film industry once the script is finished. But the development process is all about the writer, or team of writers, as the case may be. If the idea comes from a producer who's not a writer, then we'll hire a writer to collaborate with the producer in developing the story and characters. Then we wait. The process of writing and rewriting a screenplay can take years. Some scripts go through dozens of drafts and several writers.

Why? Because the film industry is story driven. For all the hype about computer-generated imagery (CGI), visual effects, and 3-D, every movie stands or falls on the basis of one factor: rich, believable characters that people can care about. Without great characters you have no story, and without a story, you have no film. Peter Jackson's *The Lord of the Rings* trilogy may have been a fantastic example of technical filmmaking, but if he hadn't made you care about Frodo, Aragorn, and the rest, it wouldn't have mattered. We spend years and a lot of money in development trying to get the characters just right.

With development there is no guarantee that the script will produce a successful movie no matter how many writers you hire. For example, the movie version of *The A-Team* spent ten years in development and went through an incredible eleven writers—five solo writers and three two-writer teams. Yet it produced a disappointing performance at the box office. Sometimes that's just how it goes in this business.

You are collaborating with God on the script of your life. You won't have eleven writers or five or even three. There's just you and the Lord, working together to craft your story, day by day. This screenplay is the plan for how you will get from where you are in your career today to where you want to be tomorrow. Just as a screenwriter sweats through multiple drafts trying to perfect his characters, God is working to help you perfect your character—your ability to manage people, create relationships, help others, act based on integrity, and so on. To achieve this, he will always steer you into *conflict*.

Conflict is the key to everything in drama, whether it's film, live theater, fiction, or television. Take characters that we can relate to, put them in situations that seem impossible to get out of, and you've got conflict. Conflict is the heart of storytelling; without it, what would the characters do? Characters in conflict have to overcome obstacles, defeat enemies, come to terms with their own demons, and take great risks when the stakes are high. That's what makes drama worth watching.

What great movie hero do you know who didn't experience conflict? Luke Skywalker discovers that Darth Vader is his father and battles his own dark side in the original *Star Wars* trilogy. Mookie contests with everyday racism in *Do the Right Thing*. Ripley fights an unstoppable alien and the destructive politics of her own company in the *Alien* franchise. Take any successful form of drama and you will find conflict shaping the characters, forcing them to confront evil and overcome their own limitations. No conflict means no story.

In your script, God will do the same with you. That is why not everything comes easily in your career. That is why you will experience setbacks and run face-first into walls. If everything came easily, how would you grow and develop the skills and wisdom you need to succeed?

For years, I pondered this issue. I wondered why God needed us to serve him at all. He created everything. Why does he need me or you to fulfill his plan for the world? Couldn't he just wave his hand and create the world that he envisions? Why ask us to serve and then put us through trial and tribulation? It didn't make sense until I thought about the idea of God as a storyteller, and then it occurred to me—he is making us stronger and better by allowing us to face conflict, overcome obstacles, and learn from failures. Remember what 1 Corinthians 10:13 says: "No test or temptation that comes your way is beyond the course of what others have had to face. All you need to remember is that God will never let you down; he'll never let you be pushed past your limit; he'll always be there to help you come through it" (The Message).

When parents give their children absolutely everything, what type of adults do those children typically become? More often than not, they are spoiled, helpless, and messed up, because they never had to endure hardship and hone their character. Children do not mature if their parents do everything for them; the best you can do as a parent is teach your children in order to mold their values and then let them go. What happens to them from there has to be their choice. We must all walk our own path, free to choose, make terrible mistakes, and recover from them.

God is our Father and we are his children. We are made in his image with the free will to choose our destiny. If he were to simply order our lives to change in the blink of an eye or to remake this world as an earthly paradise, we would be as helpless and dysfunctional as those spoiled children of rich parents. We would be his puppets. That's not what God wants for us. He helps us write our script so that we have the chance to work hard, surmount barriers, and become stronger. That is why, I believe, he calls us to his service and writes a script with highs and lows, conflict and resolution. In struggling and finding our way so that we can serve him, we come into our own.

EVERY SCREENPLAY IS CONSTRUCTED on a three-act structure. During Act One, the characters are introduced, the problem or conflict established, and situations set up that will have to pay off in Act Three. Act Two is where the story plays out and various plot points come and go. Act Two is the most challenging act, because it's difficult to weave all the plot and character threads together. This is where the story can begin to wander and lose momentum. That's why crafting an Act Two with energy and motion is critical. In Act Three, the story reaches its climax. The good guy and bad guy have their final confrontation, the zombies are killed, and order is restored from chaos . . . at least, until the sequel. A great deal of time and effort goes into making sure that each of those acts and the characters who inhabit them are as compelling and interesting as possible.

When you see that clearly, you will begin to recognize the highs and lows that are also a part of your career story. All of us, myself included, get impatient when it comes to our careers. It's tempting to flip fifty pages ahead in the script to the time when you've reached your dreams and accomplished your Big Idea. Not so fast. If you get caught up in a future you haven't even created yet, you'll skip right over the lessons and the people who will help you get there . . . and you won't ever get there. See the script unfolding and stay within it. That's the only way to guarantee that you're on God's schedule.

These are the three acts of your career story:

- FIRST ACT: This act begins when you start your career in an entry-level position. You're discovering the realities of performing your duties in the real world, learning about people, and becoming familiar with what it means to operate as a Christian within your profession. You're finding out who the important players in your life are— boss, peers, and enemies—and what opportunities might lie ahead for you.

- SECOND ACT: Just as in a film, this is the long-drawn-out act in which all the action takes place. During your lengthy second act, you're mastering the finer points of your work, enduring some failures, learning some hard lessons, piling up some triumphs, forging long-term relationships with key allies, and probably scoring a few promotions as well. You may well change companies more than once, because your story is not limited to your work with Company A; it follows you as you migrate to the next big opportunity.

- THIRD ACT: You reach the climax of your career story and the door opens to the opportunity that got you into this profession in the first place. That might mean being named CEO or senior partner, starting your own medical practice or being named head coach, landing a *New York Times* best seller or being elected to Congress. Whatever it is, Act Three comes when you reach the mountaintop. The rewards and expectations are equally great. This is your time to have a dramatic impact on the world on God's behalf, then to wind down your career in a graceful denouement. Retirement. Closing credits roll.

Of course, there are other ways your story can play out. You might reach the peak of your career at age forty-five, and then quit, reinvent yourself, and do something completely different. It happens all the time. In that case, you would go back to the first act, but with more experience, contacts, and wealth as well as a clearer idea of your talents and passions. There are as many different stories as there are people, and it is largely up to you to decide how your story plays out. Just as actors in a movie have to act, so do you. In order for your story to move forward, you've got to take action. I wish we all could just sit around and wait for God to tell us what was going to happen next, but that's not how life works. We've got to step out on faith and move in the direction we are being led.

This is where the conflict begins. Conflict between our work and our faith makes both stronger, and allowing that tension to exist helps advance our story. But it is definitely a challenge.

For me, the challenge is most apparent in the daily pursuit of my goals. When I get to the office I might be looking at my slate of development projects and then think about when the time when my contract will be up for renewal. The challenge to my faith comes when I say, "God, how am I going to get another movie made so I can validate my place at the company?" I have plenty of ambition, but sometimes I question if I have enough talent to be successful at this job. There are days and weeks like that.

But when I allow myself to become fearful, frustrated, and short-tempered about such times, I am more likely to take my eye off the ball and not do my best work. What else can you do to ensure that you are doing your best work in collaborating with God on your career story? Some suggestions straight from the unofficial Hollywood handbook on screenwriting:

- SHOW, DON'T TELL. For screenwriters, this means it's far better to use visuals to tell a part of the story than to have a character rattle off a long expository speech that leaves the audience yawning. For you, it means that rather than tell people how you intend to act at work, just do it. As I said before, talk is cheap. Your actions will speak for themselves.

- BE BOLD AND CREATIVE. The movie world doesn't need another movie about a hard-edged cop who plays by his own rules. It needs daring, original ideas and fresh characters. Your career needs the same. Emulate people who know the business and learn how to execute the fundamentals, but beyond that, get creative. Figure out ways you can make your position your own. When you're starting out and you're low person on the totem pole, find ways to add value. Don't assume that having an impact means waiting until you have title and position.

- LESS IS MORE. This is a common note in the development process. It means that when a writer has a choice between delivering a message in fifty words or in three words and a smoldering look, fewer words does the trick every time. It allows the director to use his art to convey the idea, and gives the person watching the end product the freedom to use his or her imagination. Great horror films work the same way; how much more terrifying was *Alien* because you barely saw the monster until the very end? In your career, less is also more. Not less effort, but less self-promotion. Don't worry about getting credit. Follow God, do the work, and the credit will come.

- MASTER THE BASICS. To be taken seriously as a screenwriter, you must know the essential, universal rules of scripts and storytelling. If you don't know what an establishing shot is, don't know basic screenplay format, don't understand the role of the protagonist, and can't create a clear plot point (the moment when the story switches from one act to the next), then you won't be very successful. Master the essential basics of your career. If you're an engineer working in R&D or manufacturing, learn everything about every step of the manufacturing process. If you're in marketing, become an expert on the audience you are selling to. Become a master in the universe of your job.

- LISTEN. One of the worst sins a screenwriter can commit is not knowing how people actually speak. I've read some terrible dialogue in my time. Good writers write dialogue that sounds natural and reflects the authenticity of real life. In your career, you learn by listening. Establish relationships with people who know the ropes, then listen to them. Don't try to show them how smart or clever you are! Just listen. Oliver Wendell Holmes said, "It is the province of knowledge to speak, and it is the privilege of wisdom to listen." Amen to that.

- SWEAT THE DETAILS. Typos and other errors can sink a script if the screenwriter is an unknown. Mistakes mark you as unprofessional and therefore not worth a busy executive's or agent's time. You should worry as much about precision and accuracy in your work. Even if you're at the bottom and a task seems trivial, it's important to someone. Do it better than well. Do it perfectly. You'll train yourself to deliver excellence on a deadline and your career will become better because of it.

* * *

BACK WHEN I WAS a student at USC, my major was business and my emphasis was entrepreneurship. My senior thesis for the entrepreneurship program was a business plan for an entertainment company. I had to come up with a company to model my fictitious business after, and I chose to interview Tracey Edmonds at Edmonds Entertainment. She had a dynamic entertainment company with many facets: film, TV, music, management, recording studio, real estate, etc. A friend of a friend knew her personally and was nice enough to put in a good word, and I was able to interview Tracey. She was incredibly gracious and gave me invaluable insight and knowledge about the business. So I wrote my business plan and that was that.

Until, of course, a few years later when Tracey remembered me from our interview and ended up giving me my first junior executive job. I realize now that by bringing Tracey and me together back in 1998, God was setting up a situation in my life that wasn't going to pay off until much later. But it did pay off and my job at Edmonds Entertainment was my entry into development.

Remember, when you are in the middle of your story, you can't see the twists and turns and where they will lead you. Like all of us, you are trapped in the moment, and while you can look back at your experiences and use them to predict possible outcomes in the future, you can't know how things will turn out. What might appear to be a terrible setback in Act One may be something God is using as a setup to bless you in Act Two. The challenge is not to write your faith out of your script during the downtimes. When things are going badly in your life, there will be a temptation to believe your faith is powerless over your circumstances. But just as Rocky didn't give up on his training when the fight got tough, don't give up on your faith. It will see you through. God already knows how your story will end. Even if it includes hardships and difficulties, as long as you maintain your trust you gain the victory that counts most of all: a closer, more intimate relationship with him.

How do I know this? Because God regards things differently than we do. He sees the view from thirty thousand feet and sees what is ahead on every one of the twenty possible routes you could take to your destination. You know how when you use Google Earth you can see all the twists and turns in the road you're thinking of taking on your vacation? In a way, that's what God does. He knows what's coming and is always preparing you for it.

The danger comes when you think you know better than God and end up taking shortcuts. It's one thing to know that God has a plan for you. It's another to really believe it and let that truth drive your actions, especially when there may be intense pressure to do otherwise. I know that there are many people who have abandoned their principles under difficult circumstances. Sadly, in doing so they got detoured from the blessings that God was setting up for them.

When you see others getting the opportunities that you feel you deserve, or making big money while you're scraping by, it's tempting to stop believing in God's plan. We want *what* we want *when* we want it. You have to remind yourself—every day if necessary—that life is a marathon, not a sprint. Look at the people who pursued temporary wealth in schemes with companies like Enron. Sure, they got rich in the short term, but where are they now?

What matters is not where you are today, but what kind of person God is shaping you to become in preparation for the time when he brings his vision for your life to fruition. Keep your eyes straight ahead and focus on becoming the best possible professional and Christian. Let God take care of the future.

When I met with Tracey Edmonds as a student, I knew that was part of God's process. I had no notion of how it would play out, but because I trust the Lord I made sure I conducted myself appropriately. If I hadn't made an impression as someone of passion, desire, and principles, I doubt Tracey would have remembered me four years later. If she hadn't, who knows? I might never have landed that first job. I might be in another line of work. But she did remember me, and an early plot thread resolved itself to my benefit later on when I had forgotten all about it.

When was the last time you said, "What do you want, Lord?" If God has other plans in mind for you, will you hear them? Will you be open to them? Do you want to succeed more than you want God's will in your life? Let's face it, there are days when we have no idea what God is doing. Faith is tough. Jesus struggled with it. He prayed in Gethsemane, "My Father, if there is any way you can get me out of this . . ." But in the end, his words were, "Thy will be done." God doesn't expect us to be perfect, but he does ask us to trust him.

* * *

FINALLY, AS YOU'RE WORKING on your script, you must know your moral premise and live by it. In his book *The Moral Premise: Harnessing Virtue & Vice for Box Office Success,* Stanley D. Williams, Ph.D., says that a popular movie always contains a moral premise that we all hold to be true. In *The Karate Kid,* it might be "Live in fear and you will die, but face your fear and you will triumph." In *Spider-Man,* part of the moral premise is "With great power comes great responsibility." When characters operate in vice (anger, revenge, lying, cheating, bullying, gossiping), bad things happen to them, and when they operate in virtue (forgiveness, love, courage, selflessness, kindness, generosity), good things come to them. Sometimes a virtuous character will fall into vice, and there is always a price to be paid before they learn, grow, and find their way back. All great characters face a struggle between their virtues and their vices: lust versus fidelity, mercy versus vengeance, and so on.

Most good movie scripts feature a powerful, universal moral premise that audience members can identify with. Your story must be built on similar bedrock. What virtue do you extol in your work and what vice do you condemn? What do you stand for and what do you stand against? The moral premise of your faith should be the arbiter of how you act in business.

For example, your moral premise could be "I will do unto others as I would have them do unto me." Why is this concept important? In business, there is tremendous temptation to operate in vice—it can be richly rewarded. Yet God has called us to a higher standard: operating in virtue. Developing a moral premise for your faith will help you keep your conduct virtuous.

Pursuing virtue doesn't undermine our effectiveness, nor does it limit our understanding of business. You should be astute enough to understand how the game is played, but at the same time say, "Lord, how do you want me to use my knowledge of the rules and of you to play this game the way you want me to?" We must each find a way to do business and love Christ at the same time. The two are not mutually exclusive. As we deal with difficult situations on the job we must ask, "How am I showing love? How am I showing understanding? How am I showing forgiveness?" I try to let these types of questions shape my deal making, hiring, creative decisions—everything I do.

This is not an easy way to conduct your career. It means holding yourself to a higher code of behavior regardless of the environment you work in. Your faith should be the cornerstone of your integrity and your integrity should be the cornerstone of your faith. When you conduct yourself in vice you will limit your potential for success in the long run. Committing yourself to virtue means some weeks, you're going to feel like you're on a treadmill making no progress. I've been there.

But in the end, God will raise you up to great things as he did Daniel.

When Darius was king of Babylon, Daniel ran afoul of him because he continued to pray to God, refusing to embrace the practice of monarch worship. Outraged, the king threw Daniel into the lions' den, presuming he would be devoured. But the next day, Daniel was alive. God had closed the mouths of the lions and protected Daniel because of the steadfastness of his faith. We have to accept that God will do the same for us if we stick to His script.

- What conflicts have marked your life and how did you handle them?

- How have they shaped your character?

- What is the moral premise at the center of your work?

- What act is your story in today?

- In the past, have you deviated from God's path because you lost faith?

- What happened when you did?

CHAPTER FIVE

GETTING NOTES

God opposes the proud,
but gives grace to the humble.
—James 4:6 NIV

My great-grandfather emigrated from Jamaica to the San Francisco Bay area before the turn of the twentieth century. Upon arriving, he became a Seventh-day Adventist. When he married my great-grandmother and had a family, he raised all his children in the faith, including my grandmother. Well, as you might expect, she raised her kids, including my mom, the same way.

I spent most of my early years under the tutelage of my uncle Dr. D. J. Williams, a legend in the Seventh-day Adventist church who started his own ministry in East

Oakland called Wings of Love Maranatha Ministries. That church was where I grew up and into my Christian faith and my life in the service of Jesus' Word. I gave my first sermon there on Youth Day when I was sixteen. I was always active at school (I was the student body president of my high school), but I was always most active in the church.

But I didn't want to make the church my life the way my uncle had done; being in the ministry was not in my heart. I wanted to make movies. People said, "DeVon, you should preach," and I said, "Thanks, but no thanks." I didn't understand at the time how ministry could coincide with my film aspirations. I thought it was an "either-or" kind of decision. My perspective was either I was pursuing film or I was going into the ministry, but I didn't have any idea how I could do both.

It didn't occur to me that my desired career in Hollywood could dovetail with my service to God, or that my career could become a ministry in itself. The difference maker for me and my perspective on ministry—the thing that helped me get to the point where I am pursuing what God has given to me—actually came from my younger brother. He attended Oakwood University, and while he was an undergraduate, he and his friends decided they wanted to stage a revival at Wings of Love (this is what passes for college-age rebellion in the Christian community!). My younger brother and I always fought growing up because we're so much alike, but he ultimately prevailed upon me to take a short break from my work and fly up to Oakland for several days to attend the revival. What I saw absolutely blew me away: four young men no older than nineteen, taking turns preaching to big, enthusiastic crowds, all of them on fire for the Lord.

While the other people were standing and swaying and singing and praising Jesus, I was pondering. I felt God saying, "DeVon, I gave you the gift of preaching. Why aren't you using it?" I replied, "But I want to be in entertainment," and God shot back, "Don't worry about that. I have given you a gift. You should use it."

As I pondered God's words, it became clear to me that while I had grown up steeped in the faith, I had left for a career in a world that was—outwardly, at least—extremely secular. Professions of faith may be common in the sports world, but they are not as common in Hollywood. The crowd with which you choose to associate—the world in which you immerse yourself—influences the path you choose to walk. Clearly, it had shaped mine.

Had I been distancing myself from my faith because deep down I had thought it would be unacceptable to be a Bible-quoting Christian in the movie business? Had I been assuming that if I "went public" with my beliefs it would hurt my chances to become successful? Perhaps I had. I wasn't even sure why. I was proud of my faith, my ministry, and my heritage. One thing became clear: I had to make a change.

I began to pray, asking God, "How do you want me to be involved in ministry?" I kept on praying after I went back down to Los Angeles and back to school. Then, about the time I was graduating from USC, I got a call from my uncle. In speaking about the ministry, he would always joke and tell me, "DeVon, you can run but you can't hide." But on this occasion he wasn't joking at all. "DeVon," he said, "I'm getting older. Can you come up and help me preach?" Okay, God, I said, that was pretty obvious.

I was involved with a church in L.A. at the time, but of course I flew up to Oakland and preached at Wings of Love. It was like coming home. I knew that God wanted me at least to be *partially* in the world of the church as a minister. In 2002, I was ordained as an elder at Wings of Love, I was 24 years old, and after that, my uncle asked if I could come up once a month and preach regularly. Since then, not only have I preached at Wings of Love but I now preach regularly in Los Angeles and all over the country.

THIS STORY IS a perfect illustration of how God reaches into our lives to subtly (and sometimes not so subtly) guide our choices in the direction that will help us become the finest people we can be. I was bound and determined to go to Hollywood; pursuing ministry as any sort of vocation was of no interest to me. But God had other plans. I think he wanted me to have an anchor to my faith and the commitments that it represents, even as I went to seek success in the movie business. That's why he put obvious signs in my path.

When I didn't pay attention to what people were saying to me, he brought me to my younger brother's revival and spoke to me. When I still turned away, he sent the call from my uncle, an appeal that I simply could not refuse. Of course, God was right. My preaching and deep involvement in ministry have been a blessing and a real advantage to my career. But it took God a few tries to get his feedback through my thick young man's head. When I finally listened, doors started to open.

In the film development process, feedback takes the form of notes. Successful professionals in any business solicit feedback and take it seriously. They do not assume they have all the answers. That is no different in Hollywood. Here, there are no overnight hits. We are in the movie business because we want to make hits that make money and touch the lives of people around the world. But this is a process of collaboration and constant revision. A wise man once said, "Great movies aren't written, they're rewritten." The people who have made hit after hit for decades—Will Smith, Tom Hanks, Tom Cruise—are the ones who study the craft, know the business, stay focused, take risks, and look at the long term. They accept feedback, remain humble, and learn from their mistakes.

When a script is in development, every draft comes back to the writer and producer with many notes from the studio on characters, dialogue, pacing, structure, and a hundred other parts of the story. If you want the studio to continue funding your rewrites and eventually get your movie made, addressing notes is essential.

The notes process can be brutal, especially if you've been slaving away on a script for years and think you've finally got it just right. So you can't get proud about your work. That's not to say that a writer should cave about every point; sometimes a scene or character is worth fighting for. But in general, we expect the notes to be taken seriously and best efforts made to address them. As long as critical notes in the script remain unaddressed, the script will remain in development and the movie will not get made. That's not anyone's goal. We all want to go into production.

The process of collecting feedback—getting notes—continues even after a film is in the can. When *The Karate Kid* was wrapped and edited, we started doing test screenings in January of 2010. We ended up being the second-highest-testing movie in the history of the studio and the highest-testing family movie in the history of Columbia Pictures. But that's only part of the story. When you do a test screening for a movie like this, you test adults, teenagers, and kids. We knew the movie was going to do well with families, but we wanted to see if it would work with a general audience, people without kids.

To create a test screening, you recruit your ideal audience groups. Ours was a mix of mothers with children, families, and general moviegoers. Then you choose a location. The idea is to duplicate as closely as possible the ideal audience and market where you think your film will play well. For some movies, the sweet spot is the middle of the country. For others, you might fly to Vegas or New York. For *Karate Kid*, we tested in Burbank, California. We recruited an audience of about four hundred and showed the film.

We tested beautifully with all groups, so we knew we had a film that people would respond to. We had some notes about length (should we cut the film to come in below two hours?) and violence (we needed to edit down some violent scenes to get a PG-13 rating without damaging the integrity of the film). We ended up getting the legendary James Horner to score the film. We made some other important compromises and, when we were done, we knew we had a film that would satisfy our many constituencies.

* * *

NOTES ARE A CRITICAL part of development in the film world, and the same is true in your career. You must be able to take notes from God and from other people in order to learn and grow. God has me at Sony* as part of his divine plan for my life. I am in my position because he wants me there. I am learning many things: how to be an executive, how to manage people, and how to balance the demands of my career with the demands of my faith. But if I need to do something differently or use my talents in another way, God will send me notes to advise me of this. If I heed God's input, he will lead me on paths that will satisfy both his purpose and my ambition at the same time.

God is constantly giving us notes on our choices and the ways in which we exercise our faith. These notes can take many forms: people or events appearing serendipitously, ideas that you can't get out of your head, or sometimes literal revelations that come to you in prayer. Normally, when God sends you notes, he is trying to course-correct a part of your story, just like a studio executive will try to redirect a point in a script in development. It is up to you to be humble, accept God's notes, and act on them in good faith. This can be challenging when God's feedback contradicts something that you really want or a choice that you thought was right. But that's when you must learn to swallow your pride and pay attention. I speak from experience.

In 2003 I was working as a junior executive for Tracey Edmonds, the job I landed after I left Overbrook. The com-

---

* When I refer to working at Sony, I mean Sony Pictures Entertainment, a division of Sony Corporation.

pany had its hands in film, TV, and music, so I was learning my position, making contacts, and absorbing everything that anyone would teach me. Tracey had a "first-look" deal with Fox, which means that Fox paid all the company's development overhead and in return got an exclusive first look at any new movie ideas. Well, while I was working there, that deal expired. When you're at a company that doesn't have a first-look deal, it's hard to get films made. Agents and writers are much less likely to share material with companies that don't have a relationship with a studio. So the flow of projects slowed, and the economy (this wasn't long after the dot-com crash, remember) just made things worse.

I asked God how this was all likely to work out, but didn't really get a clear answer. I knew I was happy to be an executive. I was having fun working on TV shows, music projects, and more. It was a phenomenal classroom, but it was unclear how I was going to advance. This is when it's tempting to seize control over our future and try to make things happen. We fear that God is not real and we doubt that he has things under control.

One precept I have always lived by is that you never burn a bridge, because you never have an idea how the relationships you build today will impact you tomorrow. You should always treat whatever job you're in as a position of service, even when you think it's menial or meaningless. You have no idea who is watching or how what they think of you will come into play down the line. In the Parable of the Talents, the master says to the servant, "You have been faithful over a few things, now I will make you ruler over many." We must stay faithful; while I was feeling lost at Overbrook, if I had let my depression become toxic, I'm certain I would not have had the opportunities I have enjoyed.

One morning, out of the blue, I got a call from Toby Jaffe, executive vice president of production at MGM. I didn't know who he was, but he knew me. Teddy Zee, a producer who had been at Overbrook, had noticed my work and my passion, and when Toby asked him for someone who might be a good fit at MGM, Teddy gave him my name. They were looking for an executive and wondered if I would be interested in coming in for an interview.

You see how God works? I wasn't shopping around; I was just doing my job.

I had never wanted to be a studio executive. My goal was to be a producer—that was my sole focus. I didn't know how I was going to make it happen, but that's what I wanted. I didn't think a studio executive had a life; all they did was read scripts. I wanted more balance. But then it occurred to me that this might be God sending me a note. Perhaps there was a reason why he was providing me this opportunity. So I agreed to an interview.

I didn't want anyone at Edmonds to know what was going on, so on Friday it was business as usual. Things were very casual, so I wore jeans. I figured I could go home and change before my interview. But my morning meeting with Tracey ran long and I had to choose. Should I go home and change and be late, or be on time and do the interview in jeans? I decided I would make a better impression by being on time than by being well dressed.

So I walked into the lobby of MGM—gold lion, marble lobby like you're in Las Vegas—in my jeans and cotton shirt. I met with Toby and Elizabeth Cantillon, executive vice president of production, and it was very relaxed and con-versational. We talked about life at a studio, they gave me two scripts to read, asked me to make some notes and come back for another meeting. Coming out of the meeting, I still wasn't sure I wanted to be a studio executive. But I did the notes. Then I found out through the grapevine that MGM had been searching for a black executive. There are very few studio executives of color, even now, and there were none at MGM. They were just coming off *Barbershop* and they had no diversity within the company. They wanted to find out who they could hire who had a good reputation and some ability. They had met with every available black executive in town, people much more senior than me. Friends told me not to get my hopes up. I replied, "God is in control. What's meant to be will be."

Did I care that race was a consideration? Not at all. Op-portunity is opportunity; it's all about what you do with it that counts. I went to the follow-up interview with Michael Nathanson, the head of production. (This time, I wore a suit and tie.) Toby had told me, "If Michael likes you, we're going to do this."

I don't know if the pressure got to me or what, but I was a wreck. My palms sweated, I didn't complete my thoughts, and I felt like I was dropping the ball. The opportunity was mine to lose, and I felt I was losing it. So what if I wasn't sure I wanted to work at a studio? I wanted to have the option! But I figured that if the Lord wanted me to have this job, I would have it.

I must have done better than I thought, because Toby called me after I left and said that Michael liked me. The job was mine if I wanted it. I asked him if I could sleep on it. A door was opening in front of me, but I still wasn't sure it was the one that I wanted to walk through.

I slept on it, and then next day I talked to one of my dearest friends in the business, who said, "If you ever get offered a studio job, take it. A studio job is like grad school. You work on a lot of movies and meet a lot of people."

I looked at the progression of events and I could see God's hand orchestrating things: Teddy Zee talking to Toby, going to the meeting in jeans and striking a casual tone that allowed Toby and Elizabeth to get to know me, Michael liking me in spite of my clumsy interview. This was a leap of faith on their part; I had never worked on a movie before. If they could take that leap, so could I. I called later that day to accept.

I HAVE NO DOUBT that God was giving me one big note when he steered me toward a studio job. But listening to the feedback was up to me. It was counter to everything I had seen myself doing; the story I was writing was different. But in the end, I had to have faith that God knew better than I did. If I hadn't been willing to take his note, change my plans, and get outside my comfort zone, who knows where I might be? Quite possibly out of the business. One thing you can say about the great leaders in the Bible, from Joseph to Paul: they never played it safe.

God's notes will always guide you toward situations that will test you and help you become a greater person and a better Christian. They may not line up perfectly with your plans, but that's where faith comes into play. Are you defensive—or willing to listen? How ready are you to collaborate with God on your path? Odds are, when God sends you a note, he is trying to put you in position to learn more about your craft and become more of an asset to your employer and to him. But first you have to recognize a note for what it is, then be willing to listen.

Sometimes it's easy to see God's feedback. My out-of-the-blue call from MGM couldn't have been more obvious if God had put a hundred-foot neon sign on my front lawn that read, "DeVon, I want you to change course." That kind of note is hard to miss, but they're not all that cut-and-dried. These are some of the other ways God can send you notes about your career:

- You don't get a position or a deal that you wanted badly, even though you thought you had it locked up. God holds the copyright on "Be careful what you wish for." If he prevents you from getting something that you were aching for, it's because it would not have turned out to be the blessing you expected.

- Your instincts set off alarm bells about a company, a person, or a decision. Trust them. Gut feelings and intuition are God whispering in our ears that something's not right.

- You receive advice from someone you didn't expect. When it's from your boss or your supervisor, that's normal. But when a client, vendor, or competitor does it, that's especially notable. Be sure to listen.

- You happen upon an article, blog post, or TV segment about a career-related subject that's been on your mind. This happens to me frequently: I'll be thinking about a project, a company, or a person and seemingly out of nowhere, I stumble upon relevant, useful information about that same project, company, or person. Carl Jung called these "synchronicities." I call them God getting our attention.

- You get a performance review that takes you by surprise. Notes don't get much more obvious than this. If your review isn't as good as you expected, that's often a very direct message from the Lord to either step up your efforts or rethink what you're doing.

When you get a note from God, pay attention. In Hollywood, a studio will fund the development of a screenplay as long as the writer, producers, and/or director are working in good faith to fix problems and move the project forward. But sometimes, creative teams fail to address the notes that I or other studio execs give them.

It's not always from a lack of trying; sometimes notes are difficult to execute. In other instances, the creative team genuinely disagrees with the notes and feels the project has been in development for too long without moving any closer to production. In any case, notes are being given, rewrites are being done, and the problems persist. There are times when no amount of notes or months of hard work can fix a script. This usually happens because a concept or story is fatally flawed. Whatever the reason, if this failure continues, development will stall. When that happens, the studio may choose to stop funding development. This is when a project is on the brink of falling into what we call "Development Hell," which I'll talk about in the next chapter.

God will give you notes on your character and on the areas of your life that need to be improved. If you're not making progress in life or in your career in the way you had in mind, you should be ready to humble yourself, absorb the lesson, and take action. But it is always your choice. If you fail to see the note or refuse to listen to it and remain stubbornly on the same course, then God will give you the same note again in a different way. The next version of the note might be less subtle and more disruptive, because God will do whatever it takes to get your attention.

- What notes has God given you on your career so far?

- How did you respond to them?

- What has happened in the past when you ignored God's notes?

- How have you benefited from following God's feedback, even if it was counter to what you wanted at the time?

- How has following the feedback from other people made you better at what you do?

- Are you in a position to be a source of notes to others? If so, how do you deliver your feedback?

CHAPTER SIX

DEVELOPMENT HELL

It is easy to go down into Hell;
night and day the gates of dark Death stand wide;
but to climb back again, to retrace one's steps
to the upper air—there's the rub, the task.
—Virgil, *The Aeneid*, Book VI

Sometimes, we listen to our notes. We heed the feedback from God. But just as with Hollywood screenplays, life can stall even when we are putting our best foot forward. We call this Development Hell.

In film, nobody wants to be stuck in Development Hell. You're in limbo, stuck in a snare of conflicting egos, notes that don't get addressed, and plots that have been rewritten so many times that they don't even resemble what caught the studio's attention in the first place. There's little hope that your movie will ever get made. It's a depressing, frustrating hole in which to be trapped; you may have invested years of hard work, and for what?

Development Hell can come only after you've gone into Development and think you're on your way to the top, only to hit a patch of ice and start spinning out of control.

IN LATE 2003 I started working at MGM, and the first film I worked on was *Be Cool*, the sequel to *Get Shorty*. Following my policy of trying to add value and contribute wherever possible, I managed to make an impact despite being the lowest man on the corporate ladder. The plot of the movie hinged on a song that the young girl character sang. John Travolta's character, Chili Palmer, hears this song and it becomes a big hit in the third act of the movie. The filmmakers spent a long time looking for the song, but couldn't find anything that sounded quite right. Well, in working with Tracey Edmonds I had built a relationship with Alicia Keys's manager, so I called him. "Do you have any songs that Alicia hasn't recorded?" I asked. He sent me two, I sent them along to the *Be Cool* music supervisors and producers, and they liked one of them. It became "the song."

It was the perfect validation for me—there was already another junior executive working on the film, so to pull in a third executive was uncommon. I could have been the tenth exec on the movie, it wouldn't have mattered; I was just happy to be part of something and learn. And what a blessing that God had allowed me to develop relationships at Edmonds Entertainment that helped me make an impact at MGM. I was able to leverage those relationships to contribute and to build my relationship with Elizabeth Cantillon, who had given me the opportunity to work on the film. I was happy and off to a very promising start.

But then the rumors began. About six months after I started, word got around that MGM was trying to sell the company. After a while, it looked like Time Warner (TW) was going to buy MGM. This was not good. TW had already bought a lot of the MGM film library, which included classics like *The Wizard of Oz* and *Gone with the Wind*. Rumor was that if TW bought MGM, they would consolidate the film library and shut the rest of the company down. I, along with thousands of others, would be on the street looking for work.

I asked God, "How is this going to work? As soon as I get here, the studio is selling?" I tried not to fret and to focus on the work, but that was easier said than done. The idea of having to potentially start all over again wasn't only frightening, it was terrible. I couldn't make plans, and I couldn't take action. I felt directionless. No one at the office knew what was going to happen, and there was a lot of anxiety. "God," I said, "how can you take me away from Tracey and lead me here, only to have me lose my job?" I didn't understand any of it.

Eventually, the general consensus was that it wasn't a question of if MGM was going sell but to whom and when. I figured I was going to have to get a job in a market where there weren't any. I knew I couldn't sit back and wait around. Faith without works is dead, so I had to do my part in order for God to step in and do his part.

As it happened, in the summer of 2004 Will and JL, my old bosses at Overbrook, were holding a fund-raiser for Barack Obama's Illinois Senate campaign. I knew that Overbrook had a first-look deal with Sony, so it was likely that the chairman and presidents of production at Sony would be there. So I found a way to pay for the $1,000 ticket.

The plan seemed to work. It was a wonderful event with lots of people and an elegant ambience. It's funny in hindsight; there was a moment when now-President Obama walked by and was greeting people, and I was far less interested in meeting the man who would become our first African-American president than I was in tracking down and meeting Amy Pascal, Matt Tolmach, and Doug Belgrad of Sony Pictures. After all, my whole reason for attending the event was to make contact with them.

I found them, walked right up, and introduced myself. There was no room for nerves or chickening out; if I wanted God to bless me I had to put works behind my faith! Long story short, they were great and were kind enough to indulge me in conversation. After a few minutes, I thanked them and walked away. That was my big Hail Mary pass. I was trying to set the stage for the job hunt I felt was coming and hoped that down the road they would somehow remember me.

September came, and with it an announcement that in an eleventh-hour move, Sony had swooped in with some equity investors to purchase MGM, despite all the signs that the sale was sure to go to Time Warner. I sighed. Okay, that was that. At least I had some concrete information. Now that a deal had been made, everyone involved had to wait on the Federal Trade Commission to approve the deal, which would probably take months.

At Thanksgiving that year, my family went on retreat. We were all sitting around in a circle having evening worship, and we went around with each of us saying what we were thankful for and what we were praying for. I told my family that I was praying and believing that God would give me a job at Sony. That night, we all wrote down our prayer requests. Mine was simple: *Lord, thy will be done and I pray that your will is pointing in the direction of Sony.* If all I got was a severance package from MGM, that wouldn't be bad at all, yet if I got a job at Sony, that would be incredible. It would allow me to continue developing as a studio executive, something I was really beginning to enjoy.

But I just couldn't take much more of limbo.

January 2005 came; we were releasing *Be Cool* in March. The Sony*-MGM sale was close to final, and there was a major meeting with the executives of both companies. One of the people in that meeting was Elizabeth, who was a close friend of Amy Pascal. After that meeting, Elizabeth called me down to her office and closed the door. "I just got back from the meeting at Sony," she said. "I have a message for you from Amy Pascal: Don't look for a job. You have one."

I was stunned. I wanted to do a holy dance all the way down the hall, but I waited until I got back to my office and then I started wondering. Elizabeth and I were going to be the only execs from our department to survive the transition? How was that possible? I understood why Elizabeth was going, but I was the person with the least seniority in my entire division. I had been the last person hired. Yet I

---

* To be clear, Sony Corporation, not Sony Pictures Entertainment, bought MGM.

was going to make the cut? All I could say was "Thank you, Jesus!" I knew he had intervened.

How ironic is it that I had started my journey with Will and JL at Overbrook, and now I was going to be at Sony, where their production company was housed? It was clearly part of a greater design that the Lord was bringing me back into relationship with them again. You can't plan that.

IN YOUR CAREER, DEVELOPMENT Hell occurs when you reach a place where you stop progressing and might even feel as if things are going in reverse. Your company might be for sale the way mine was, and you might not know if your position will survive the sale. You may have taken on a big challenge and performed up to expectations but the promotion you thought was coming never came. You may be on the verge of being downsized because of the economy. Or your passion for your work might have simply run dry and you don't know how to get it back. When you start to wonder why you're putting in the long hours, when you get sick of waiting for your time to come, when you lose perspective, when it feels like life is on "repeat" . . . there's a parking spot in Development Hell with your name on it.

Most of us have been in this position at one time or another. Your career is a three-act script, and in Hollywood the second act is the longest and potentially the most boring. If a script isn't well developed to bring strong pacing and a sense of forward motion to Act Two, the entire movie can stall. The same thing can happen in your career. In Act One, when you first get a new position and possibly even begin a profession you've spent years training for, you're naturally excited. Even the mundane parts of your work are interesting for a while.

But then some time passes. Reality sinks in. You realize that you're on a long, slow road to your future. You're not going to become CEO or manage your division overnight. The duties that were interesting when you were an enthusiastic novice have become drudgery. You start to doubt that God knows what he's doing. Surely, he has bigger things in mind for you than spending ten years as a junior account executive or assistant editor?

Be careful of that sort of thinking, because it will only make the pain of Development Hell more difficult to endure. One of the important things to remember about Development Hell is that it has little to do with what your opportunities actually are at the time and everything to do with *what you perceive those opportunities to be.* When I was on pins and needles for an entire year at MGM, I didn't need to be. If I'd put my full trust in God, I would have known that he had something in mind for me. That time was a phenomenal lesson in how God works in our lives. There was the way I was perceiving things—tense, frightening, and poised on the edge of disaster—and the way things really were, which was positive and validating.

It was my choice how I chose to look at my situation.

Most of us spend some time in Development Hell; it's part of the process of building a career. We all experience an intense period of doubt, tedium, and failure as we're learning. Every single one of us faces a hard dose of reality when we move from just dreaming to being in an environment where we have to work on making our dreams come to fruition.

When you go from a university to a "real" job or from an apprenticeship to being the master, it can be a shock. You find that you're working harder than ever, sometimes without anyone to catch you when you stumble. You find that the glamour you thought your work would entail is easily balanced by routine and repetition. Or you work in your position for a year or two and wake up one day and surprise!— you've lost that lovin' feeling for the profession you once thought you would want to be in for the rest of your days.

That's normal; we're all learning about ourselves in the ultimate on-the-job training. God will steer us into circumstances that will shape our character. But the danger grows the longer we *stay* in Development Hell, because we risk sending our dreams into *turnaround*.

When a film project goes into turnaround, the studio has officially given up on it after years of development. The idea we first loved is gone and the project is dead. The studio stops paying any expenses and puts the project in turnaround so that another studio can buy it and develop it if they choose.

The longer we spend in Development Hell, the stronger the urge to put our hopes in turnaround. We want to give up. We lose faith and say, "Lord, it's not going to happen." Remember, we are stuck in the present and we tend to judge the progress we're making toward our goals by what is happening *today*. If we get the promotion today, it's time for a party. If our boss passes over us in favor of someone else, then we want to close the shades and mope. What we often lack is a *big-picture* view of things; we forget that we can't know what God has working for us in the future. It's important to retain some perspective on our suffering and to tell ourselves over and over that things can turn on a dime, and often do.

People really believe something only after the fact, and that's where faith comes in.

We don't have to know what's going to happen, we just have to trust that God will not leave us without hope.

If you are in Development Hell, don't throw in the towel. You're probably not as far away from Production as you might think. You might be just one scene away from where you want to be. Think of the bathroom scene in *The Pursuit of Happyness* where Chris Gardner had nowhere to take his little boy for the night, so they had to camp out in a subway station bathroom. That was the low point of his journey, and it would have been easy for him to say, "Enough. I quit." But if he had given up then, he would have never gotten the stock-trading job that changed his life forever. Instead, he went back into the office the next day with as much hope as he could muster, and his determination not to give up was what he needed to endure the hell he was going through.

Remember that the movie was based on a true story. Chris Gardner really faced all that fear, homelessness, and uncertainty, kept faith, and triumphed. If he could do it, so can you.

PROJECTS DON'T LANGUISH IN Development Hell because people don't like them anymore. In fact, it's usually the exact opposite. Many times it's because the studio and filmmakers can see a good idea beneath the surface of the script, but are having difficulty figuring out the story. Obviously, the idea is promising enough that the studio has spent years, effort, and money trying to crack the script. One of my bosses has been developing the classic pirate adventure story *Sinbad and the Seven Seas* for years and will not give up on it because he knows that one day it will become a movie. But sometimes a project just has to wait for that fresh perspective or big idea that will unlock its potential.

God is just like this with us: Even when we don't see the potential in ourselves, he does. No matter how much hell this life has taken us through, he knows the dream he placed with us and will not give up on us. He knows that one day our dream or idea will impact the world. But even when you accept this and you aren't ready to give up on your goal, what happens when your employer has put you in turnaround? You've gotten demoted, or worse, you've lost your job. If you've been put in turnaround through no fault of your own, it says nothing about the quality of the work you have done. The great irony (as a dear friend of mine says) is that some of the biggest hit movies were picked up out of turnaround. Being put in turnaround isn't the end of the world.

Which movies am I talking about?

How about *Forrest Gump* (grossed $677 million worldwide and won the Oscar for Best Picture)?

How about *Slumdog Millionaire* (grossed $377 million worldwide and won the Oscar for Best Picture)?

That's not good enough for you?

How about *Twilight*?

The blockbuster teen vampire romance franchise was picked up out of turnaround from Paramount. Even though the books were major best sellers, no one thought they could make the films work. So far, the *Twilight* films combined have grossed almost *$2 billion* worldwide; it's one of the most successful film franchises in history.

Want more evidence that turnaround isn't such a big deal? Well, consider that Frank Price, a famous Columbia executive, passed on *E.T. Star Wars* was passed on. The rights to *The Lord of the Rings* sold to Universal in the 1970s but New Line ended up making it with director Peter Jackson. Those three films earned seventeen Academy Awards and grossed more than $2.9 billion worldwide.

The lesson? Even if one company misses the value in a project, it doesn't mean that another won't see it and take advantage. Don't worry if one company doesn't or didn't see your value and true potential. God does. And because he does, he already has the company or opportunity that will pick you up out of turnaround and put you back on the path to even bigger success. He has you in your industry for a reason, and if things are at a seeming dead end with your current employer, it only means that greater opportunity awaits you elsewhere.

WHAT HAPPENS WHEN YOUR employer is giving you chances to advance and do your best work but you buy your own one-way ticket to Development Hell? When things stagnate, it can be because you've stopped caring about your work. You're "phoning it in" and just punching the clock. You're probably not doing what you're passionate about, and when that happens, it's virtually impossible to put the best of yourself into what you do.

As I've shared, I've had days when I felt as if there would never be another opportunity coming my way. Nobody wants to work beneath their potential; it's a miserable, lifeless way to spend a career. If that's the reason you're in Development Hell, it's time to look in the mirror. Clearly, God has a path prepared for you, but are you on it? In landing in your current position, did you pay attention to the signs that God sent indicating where and how to best use your talents? Or did you freelance, deciding that the company or line of work God was directing you toward wasn't interesting and you would rather do something else instead? That's losing faith. That's trusting in your own wisdom and placing it above the Lord's wisdom. When you do that—when you dig in your heels and resist his attempts to lead you in a certain direction—you miss out on his blessings.

In a self-created Development Hell, we have two options: *straighten up* or *get out*. Remember, God sees what is in our futures, so he knew that you would resist his will and end up in a job where you feel unhappy and directionless. Why? Because he wants you to learn something. Either you stick with your current job for a while and vow to do your best and learn whatever it has to teach, or you humble yourself, admit your error, leave your job, and turn yourself over to God's will. Pray and pay attention; he will guide you out of Development Hell.

When you finally escape, listen to your passion. We frequently forget that the passion we feel—for law or finance, teaching or repairing classic cars—is placed in us by God. Each is a spiritual seed that will one day bear fruit and bring us to the career we were meant to have. Listen to the voice of your passion and it won't lead you astray.

* * *

IS DEVELOPMENT HELL INEVITABLE? Some movies must breeze through the process without ever getting stuck in endless rewrites, right?

Sure. It happens. But it's rare. For one thing, every studio develops far more ideas and scripts than it will ever produce. We do it for a simple reason: some films won't ever pan out, and we need to have multiple projects in the pipeline so that for every three that go into turnaround, we have one or two that can move into production. So most movies at some point will wind up in Development Hell. The key question is, do they stay there? The success stories don't. They either sell to another studio that finds the combination to unlock the magic in the story, or someone at the original studio has a brilliant idea that saves the day and the project moves ahead.

You'll probably spend some time in Development Hell; most of us do. If it doesn't come in the form of missed opportunity, then it might manifest as an ethical crisis or boredom with your duties. But when you do reach that stage, the key to dealing with it is staying the course and being steadfast in your faith. The risk is that you will ditch your purpose and take shortcuts to advance by any means possible. That practically guarantees that you'll be taking up long-term residence in Development Hell, because you will not be able to receive God's blessings in the way he has planned.

If you can keep your eyes looking ahead even when the difficult times come, you will accept God's decision to put you through the purifier of Development Hell in order to mold your ambition, integrity, and perspective. Don't abandon what makes you who you are. Don't give up hope.

God will pull you out of Development Hell soon enough, and you will move ahead into the next scene of your life. You will be ready to make a powerful, lasting impact on the world.

One of the most effective tools I've discovered which can help you manage the tough times is to *remember*. We have a tendency to forget how good God has been to us. Think back over all the scenes of your life. Think about the times when you needed God the most—did he ever let you down? If you're like me, then not only did God come through for you in your past, but every time he did, he exceeded your expectations! If he did it before, then he will do it again. Let your past experiences with him bring you comfort and confidence to keep moving forward.

When you feel trapped in Development Hell, also think about steps you can take to help you manage this difficult period. Attend events where you can network with people. Take training courses to become even better at your job. Pitch your boss on a creative new idea. Take on a project no one else will accept. Propose a daring solution to a long-standing problem. These tactics all keep you on God's road while bringing new energy and purpose to your work. Keep the faith and keep your sense of perspective and, believe it or not, Development Hell will ultimately seem like time well spent.

- Are you in Development Hell now?

- Have you been in the past?

- What needs to happen to move you out of it?

- What are you doing to balance your pursuit of money with your service to God?

- Have you ever doubted that your desired career is the right one for you?

- If so, how did you resolve those doubts?

CHAPTER SEVEN

GOD'S BUDGET AND PRODUCTION SCHEDULE

Wisdom is supreme; therefore get wisdom.
Though it cost all you have, get understanding.
—Proverbs 4:7 NIV

Back when I was working for Tracey Edmonds, we were filming the pilot for *College Hill*, a reality show for BET, kind of like MTV's *The Real World* except set at black colleges and universities. For the pilot we shot at Southern University, in Baton Rouge, Louisiana. This was the first time I had ever done anything like this. Reality TV was not my forte; I was a film executive. But one of the great things about working for Tracey was I had the opportunity to learn about all aspects of entertainment. Shooting the pilot was a team effort and she asked me to come along and help out, which I was excited to do.

The production was an all-hands-on-deck operation and everyone on location (executive or not) had to pitch in. We had a shoestring budget and it was all about getting the work done—positions were irrelevant. On the first Friday there, we needed to shoot some important footage but were short one cameraman. The crew needed me to fill in and handle the camera, but the shoot was going to happen after sundown on Friday, when I observe the Sabbath. I remember thinking, "Lord, why is it the very time I have a really good opportunity, here comes the conflict?" Now I was faced with another head-on collision between my beliefs and my job.

I was really nervous because I didn't want to let anyone down. We all had sacrificed and I knew they really needed me. But I knew that helping them, no matter how noble, would cause me to go against the core beliefs of my faith. I was racked with anxiety and confusion . . . what should I do?

As I've mentioned, keeping the Sabbath is important to me. It's a constant weekly reminder that God is in control. It's kind of like giving a tithe—every time I write the check, I'm reminded of how good he really is and how much he has already blessed me. Sabbath actually makes me better at what I do, because it gives me one day to rest and recover from six days of working my crazy schedule so that I don't burn out. I try to unwind from the week and focus on communing with the Lord—prayer, Bible study, the simple quieting of the mind—and fellowshipping with my family and friends from church. When I was growing up, there were times when my mother would let me go to school functions on Friday nights, but they were few and far between; as long as we were under her roof, my brothers and I were keeping the Sabbath holy, no two ways about it.

It's one thing when we have to live by our faith because we have no choice, but it's another thing when we're out on our own and can live however we choose. When I arrived at USC, I wouldn't go to football games because most of them were on Saturday afternoons. To be a USC student and not attend football games was considered almost blasphemous, but I never did it. My first job in college was at USC Hillel, the on-campus Jewish center. That may seem odd, but I actually enjoyed it quite a bit. They had Shabbat service and dinner on Friday nights and I never had to work after sundown, so it was a good fit for me.

For a young man aspiring to live a Christian life and trying to find his way in the world, college wasn't an easy experience. It was my first time away from home; there were parties, clubs, games, and of course women. College is traditionally a time of tremendous self-exploration when everybody questions everything. I was no exception. I remember going through a tough period in my freshman year when I felt detached from everything I had come to believe in my life. I began to question everything. Who was I? Who was God? Why did I believe what I believed? Was any of it real?

Ever been there, when everything you thought you knew doesn't make as much sense as it used to? During this period, I could feel myself turning away from what I believed and how I was raised. I started going to parties on Friday nights (I didn't drink or smoke—it was enough of a transgression for me just to go out on a Friday night!). I was very aware that it was a blatant violation of my commitment. I would feel uneasy about it but just ignore the feeling.

I remember one party in particular in celebration of a USC-UCLA football game. As I was walking through the venue, hearing the music bumping, seeing the ladies dancing and everyone having a good time, I heard God clearly say, "This is not who you are."

Has this ever happened to you? God speaks to you while you are right in the middle of doing something you know deep down you shouldn't? I replied softly, "I know." He wasn't referring to the party environment; he was referring to how I was compromising my beliefs. I was ashamed. It made me sick to think that I was betraying who I really was. I had to stop. I had to stay where God put me.

So the next Friday came around and I declined to go out. I can't begin to tell you how lonely that was. Everybody was going out to have fun and I was staying behind. The loneliest times in a college dorm are weekend nights and holiday breaks. But even in the loneliness, I felt a quiet peace because I knew I was being true to who I was. In so doing I was being true to the person God had called me to be. And this peace was more valuable than the loneliness it cost me.

THAT SAME PEACE ELUDED me in Baton Rouge on that Friday afternoon. So I stepped outside the house where we were staying and called my pastor to seek counsel. I was truly conflicted. I didn't want to let my team down because they were depending on me, but I also knew I was supposed to keep the Sabbath day holy. I was very nervous about telling the cast and crew that I couldn't do the job. I worried that it would ruin my relationship with them or make me appear arrogant and holier-than-thou. Who knows, it might even have endangered my career, which was just getting started. To my frustration, my pastor left it up to me to decide.

I couldn't believe it! Aren't pastors supposed to tell us just what to do?

Only later did I come to have a deep appreciation for how he handled the situation. It helped me develop the ability to think and make spiritual decisions on my own, which are vital skills to have. I understand now that all good spiritual leaders empower their followers with the tools to help them make decisions for themselves. After a brief discussion, he asked me a simple question: "What do you value most?"

I thought deeply about the question, then I prayed. I went back inside, took a deep breath, and told the crew that I couldn't do the evening shoot. Silence. I waited for the push-back. Then someone said, "Okay. No problem, we totally understand and we'll make do." To my immense relief and gratitude, everyone was really cool about it. Someone then said something that shocked me: they asked if we could pray together. I did a mental double take; instead of being cursed out, I was being asked for prayer. So in the middle of the living room, we all stood in a prayer circle and prayed, then hugged one another, and they took off for the shoot. The next day, a close friend of mine who was part of the crew went to church with me.

That was a turning point. Before that I had been based in our office, so I could leave at sundown easily. Baton Rouge was my field test. The sky did not fall. The world did not end. The thing that I feared did not come to pass. I was surprised and delighted and grateful to God for the grace he had shown in protecting me, as he had protected Daniel. The episode gave me even more confidence in declaring my beliefs. I have never been afraid of the outcome of the conversation since that day. I've been in meetings where this issue has come up and the question has been asked, "Can't you compromise just once?" But I have never given in. If I compromise on one Sabbath for one issue, then where do I draw the line? If I can honor it when I want to and not honor it when I don't, my faith becomes a matter of convenience.

Usually we are tempted to compromise on our promises to God because there's some reward on the table. The irony is, being steadfast will yield greater rewards that will truly edify us and benefit our careers. How do I know this? Because it's happened to me. People in the business are surprised when I tell them I can't do something because of what I believe, but by doing so I let them know what I value most. In an environment where everything is negotiable, taking something off the table and making it nonnegotiable can be empowering.

Many Christians who are otherwise truly passionate about their service to the Lord are afraid to stand on their principles in their professional lives. Have you ever found yourself in that position? Have you given in? Living in service to God always comes with a cost. Have you ever considered the cost and thought that it was simply too high?

If you have, you're hardly alone. I doubt there is a single believer (me included) who hasn't failed in this regard at least once—and most likely many times. But God doesn't expect us to be perfect. Sometimes when you allow circumstances to compromise your values and regret it after the fact, you're even more motivated to obey God's will the next time you're tempted.

In the professional world, the key is to understand that most of what we think we know about business and morality is a myth. We have this Gordon Gekko image of people in business: cynical, predatory, and ruthless, ready to slit anybody's throat to make more money or climb the ladder. But for the most part, in my experience that has not been true. Even in the corner office, people are moved by kindness, honor, and ethics. The CEO is still someone who has a family and children, someone who doesn't walk into the office each morning thinking, "Who can I cheat today?" If there are people who take actions of questionable morality in their careers, it's usually not because they are bad people but because they're doing what they must to survive.

Whether you're in entertainment, finance, or technology, the demands of most careers are mental. Because of that, the doubts we face are psychological—questions of confidence, self-worth, and self-image. When we go into the professional environment, we begin to question ourselves. *Do I have what it takes? Am I good enough? Can I advance?* It is very difficult to pursue a path of success if we define that success only in terms of promotion or the title on a business card. But if you define it as "the kind of person I become in the eyes of God," success becomes achievable.

When you let God develop and produce your career by faith, you hold fast to your commitment to him. So what if you've been tempted before and failed? As my Uncle Williams used to say: "Yesterday is a canceled check, tomorrow is a promissory note, today is ready cash, use it wisely." The past is irrelevant; it's all about what you do today. Standing up for God changes how people see you. Suddenly, in a world where everything is relative, you're an absolute. You're a person of integrity, someone whose word can be trusted and, more important, someone whom God can trust. This is what God's budget for your career is all about.

THIS BOOK IS ABOUT taking the principles central to business and applying them to faith. I am trying to practice extreme faith in an extreme environment and trying to keep one from consuming the other, and in doing so attempting to demonstrate how you can move forward in your chosen industry while maintaining your faith as a strategic asset. I don't agree with the idea of segregating our work and faith lives; the two must become one. You can't play "don't ask, don't tell" with God. Your faith is the foundation of your values—the driving force behind the vision of who you are and how you operate in this world. It *must* dictate how you operate in your work. In theory, you can be secretive about your faith and still practice it, but I believe this weakens you. It's like going to the gym but not getting on any of the machines.

The essential part of producing your faith is declaring it and allowing it to live boldly through your work.

I discovered this to be true when I began examining the parallels between how a movie winds its way through development and how God takes us on a similar spiritual journey. If a project emerges from Development Hell, then the work is only beginning. It's not enough just to have a script that is in good shape; you've also got to figure out how much the movie will cost to make and how long it will take to shoot. This is called budgeting and scheduling. They are the next critical steps in getting a project from the development labyrinth into production.

A movie budget is broken down into two types of costs: above-the-line and below-the-line. Above-the-line costs are basically the amounts to be spent on the key creative elements such as main cast, script, producers, and director. Below-the-line costs are all the amounts to be spent not included in above-the-line costs, including crew, travel and living expenses, legal and accounting fees, insurance, post-production expenses, etc. A production schedule is a breakdown of the script into actual shooting days and it gives us a good idea how long it will take to film the movie. There is a direct correlation between budget and schedule: the longer the production schedule, the more the movie costs to make.

For a movie to go into production the studio, the producers, and director must all sign off on the budget and commit to the schedule. This isn't always an easy process. It can be met with much conflict because we don't always see eye to eye on how much a project should cost. Traditionally, the studio wants to make it for less while the producers and director will insist they must have more. We share a common goal—to get the movie made—but cooler heads must prevail so that we can come to an agreement or the project will stay in development.

❊   ❊   ❊

GOD HAS A BUDGET in mind for your success. It is the cost you must bear in order to live fully in his purpose. That cost might be being unable to take career shortcuts, working in a position beneath your abilities longer than you feel you should, or suffering the disapproval of those who do not welcome people of faith in the workplace. Regardless of the cost, paying it is never easy, yet unless you bear the cost and accept God's budget, you will not progress in your true purpose.

God wants your life and career to be a box office hit (metaphorically speaking). There is nothing that would make him happier than to take your career out of development and fast-track it into production. When you are in production you will be of even greater benefit to him.

We serve a God who has a plan for us. As part of that plan he has taken the time to prepare a budget and schedule for our careers. He knows when our career will be ready to enter production, what it will cost us, and how much time will be required to produce true success in our lives. If we believe this to be true, then the next logical question is, what do we have to do to go into production?

Just as budgeting a script isn't an arbitrary process, God's plan for your production isn't random either. He's looked at your future and seen the tremendous potential you possess. The budget he's prepared for your success takes this into account.

Unfortunately, we often argue with God because we have our own ideas about what success should cost and how long production should last. There are things we don't want to do and things we don't want to give up. We aren't willing to agree on what it will cost to get our careers made, and then we get upset when the Lord shows us how long it will take to produce the level of success we desire. We want it cheap and we want it now!

Before we can move closer to production we must come to an agreement with God and sign off on his budget. God's budget always features specific line items:

1. FAITHFULNESS

As Jesus went on from there, two blind men followed him, calling out, "Have mercy on us, Son of David!" When he had gone indoors, the blind men came to him, and he asked them, "Do you believe that I am able to do this?" "Yes, Lord," they replied. Then he touched their eyes and said, "According to your faith will it be done to you."

—Matthew 9:27–29 NIV

Trusting in the limitless power of God is a fundamental requirement of production. We must believe that our circumstances do not restrict God's ability to bless us. The only thing that restricts us is our lack of faith in him. Big faith equals big blessings.

2. OBEDIENCE

If you fully obey the Lord your God and carefully follow all his commands I give you today, the Lord your God will set you high above all the nations on earth. All these blessings will come upon you and accompany you if you obey the Lord your God.

—Deuteronomy 28:1–2 NIV

Binding yourself to a God-centered code of obedience is a necessary cost of living in faith. We must all make decisions of obedience to him about what we stand for—and will not stand for. As Senate Chaplain Peter Marshall famously said in his session-opening prayer in 1947, "Give to us clear vision that we may know where to stand and what to stand for, because unless we stand for something, we shall fall for anything." What things are nonnegotiable? What are the areas in which God is calling you to be more obedient?

3. SACRIFICE

So here's what I want you to do, God helping you: Take your everyday, ordinary life—your sleeping, eating, going-to-work, and walking-around life—and place it before God as an offering. Embracing what God does for you is the best thing you can do for him. Don't become so well-adjusted to your culture that you fit into it without even thinking. Instead, fix your attention on God. You'll be changed from the inside out. Readily recognize what he wants from you, and quickly respond to it. Unlike the culture around you, always dragging you down to its level of immaturity, God brings the best out of you, develops well-formed maturity in you.

—Romans 12:1–2 The Message

The value of our faith should not simply be the comfort that it brings us or the joy and peace we get in communion with and service to the Lord. That value is also measured by what we are willing to sacrifice for our beliefs. What we have is worth what we are willing to pay for it. If we are willing to compromise in public on the things that make our faith meaningful in private, that speaks volumes about the lack of authenticity of our faith. Everything goes up for grabs. American theologian Tryon Edwards captures my view beautifully in a quote from the *Forbes Scrapbook of Thoughts on the Business of Life,* Vol. 2: "Compromise is but the sacrifice of one right or good in the hope of retaining another—too often ending in the loss of both." Commit to a career built on sacrifice, not compromise.

4. HUMILITY

Do you want to stand out? Then step down. Be a servant. If you puff yourself up, you'll get the wind knocked out of you. But if you're content to simply be yourself, your life will count for plenty.

—Matthew 23:12 The Message

This Scripture says it all.

5. SUBMISSION

Submit yourselves, then, to God. Resist the devil, and he will flee from you.

—James 4:7 NIV

We have to give ourselves over to God's authority. We have to let him develop and the produce the story he wants from our lives.

In life, we do our share of wrong. We're often guilty of not paying the cost God wants from us for the life he's given us so generously. So if we sign off on his budget, we must demonstrate it by our actions.

For me, the cost of maintaining my identity as a devout servant of God while pursuing an ambitious career path has been to adhere firmly to my Christianity. That is the payment I owe to God for giving me my life, my health, my talent, my family, everything that I have and am.

This was what my *College Hill* experience was about. I was willing to be obedient to who he called me to be and put his will over mine. That was one way to communicate to him that I'm willing to accept the cost of becoming who he wants me to be regardless of any personal discomfort that might result.

GOD'S PRODUCTION SCHEDULE FOR our careers is quite simple and can be summed up quickly starting with this verse:

> *Let us not become weary in doing good,*
> *for at the proper time we will reap a harvest*
> *if we do not give up.*
> —Galatians 6:9 NIV

When God puts us in production, we are officially on the path that will lead us even closer to our purpose. But understand this: Being in production is tough, grueling work.

Some of the most elaborate movie productions are scheduled to film over many months, shooting twelve to thirteen hours a day, five to six days a week. It's one thing to start out filming a movie with a bang on day one, but what happens when you're on day 65 of a 137-day shoot when the energy is low and the frustration is off the charts? That's another thing entirely. The more intricate the production, the longer the schedule. God alone knows how long we will need to be in production to bring him glory and produce sustainable success.

When we face a time line only God can know, the primary qualities that serve us well are patience and trust. Patience does not mean simply waiting passively, but understanding that it will take years of being in production to fully manifest our potential. As we are in production we can use the days to master skills, learn judgment and leadership, and educate ourselves in the tools and technologies that enable us to perform our work at the highest levels.

However, no film will go into production if everyone involved (the studio, producers, director) does not sign off on the schedule. The door will simply close, because the risk of failure is too great without a strong collaboration between the studio and the filmmakers. If that rapport and trust aren't there before filming begins, it will be very hard to establish it once production starts. When that happens, the integrity of the production can be jeopardized and the risk of a financial and artistic failure skyrockets. God's schedule for our careers is about establishing a collaborative partnership with us so that our faith can produce the best possible result.

Ironically, if God were to reveal to us his full schedule,

most of us wouldn't accept it. Why? Because we wouldn't want to commit to how long real success typically takes. Remember the Word says, "The race is not given to the swift." As I mentioned in my guiding principles, we need to determine how committed we truly are to attaining God's will for our careers regardless of time. I can't stress this enough. A commitment to success is not conditional. If God has called you to do it, then you should give yourself over to that process completely, with your heart, mind, and spirit.

In Hollywood, budgeting and scheduling are accomplished only with a great deal of compromise. The studio and filmmakers each state what they need to get from the process, and they meet in the middle as best they can. In the same manner, there is nothing wrong with going to God with your desired production schedule and doing everything you can to implement it.

I remember in my early twenties I wrote down that I wanted to become a vice president by the time I was thirty. This was my production schedule. In my mind that meant I wanted this to happen no later than the day I turned thirty. Well, guess what? My thirtieth birthday came and I wasn't a VP. I was devastated and upset and I felt like a complete failure. Obviously, I wasn't a failure at all; I was doing absolutely fine in my career regardless of the title I had. But because I had manufactured this expectation, when I didn't reach it, I was deeply disappointed. Now I realize that God was revealing a number of important lessons to me through that experience.

First, he took me to task on my faith. How could I let something as trivial as not getting a title get me so bent out of shape? I was behaving like a spoiled child. Second, if I would just stay faithful and trust him, he would bring me into the position at the time when it would serve him best. Last, he used this incident as an opportunity to change my perspective. See, I thought my production schedule would be complete if I could get promoted by the time I turned thirty. Yet God revealed to me how off base I was in my thinking.

The kicker was that he allowed me to get the VP promotion about six months after my thirtieth birthday, but he then revealed to me that my production schedule wasn't close to being over—in fact, it hadn't even begun yet.

God sometimes will give us what we think we want to show us how different it is from what we need. Now that I had the promotion (after much self-inflicted anxiety), what I really needed was to give myself over to God's schedule and trust that he knew best.

Don't be like I was—so intent on when a certain reward or opportunity should arrive that you become devastated if things don't transpire when you want them to. Be bold enough to request your ideal schedule from God, but be confident enough in him to agree to his schedule even if it differs from the time line you've had in your mind.

Maybe you are struggling with not wanting to fully commit to a career path because you're afraid it will take longer than you desire. Talk to God about it. Be open and honest about your fears. He will listen and help you feel more settled in your choice. Also, talk to someone who's done or is doing what you want to do, because it will help you see that many of your worst fears are illusory.

God greatly desires for us to be successful in this world, and he knows that can occur only when the time is right and the cost buys what he intends. Both the spiritual and practical approaches to budgeting and scheduling work hand in hand to help guide you to where God's always wanted you to be.

- What other costs do you think God is asking you to bear?

- Are you willing to pay the cost of your success or are you avoiding it?

- What are your proficiencies?

- What skills are most valuable to your employer? To God?

- What is your time frame for reaching your career goal? What happens if you don't reach your goal in your time frame? How will you respond?

CHAPTER EIGHT

IT'S ALL ABOUT CASTING

People are like stained-glass windows.
They sparkle and shine when the sun is out,
but when the darkness sets in, their true beauty
is revealed only if there is a light from within.
—Elisabeth Kübler-Ross, *To Live Until We Say Good-Bye*

Bishop T.D. Jakes has always been one of my favorite preachers. The only reason I still have a VCR at home is that my favorite sermon of his is available only on VHS tape. (Maybe one of these days I'll have it converted to DVD.) His word has always impacted me. Back when I was working with Tracey Edmonds, I was always trying to figure out ways I could make movies with him.

When I got to Sony, to my surprise, I found out that Michael Lynton, the chairman and chief executive officer of Sony Pictures Entertainment, was making a first-look production deal with Bishop. His 2004 film, *Woman, Thou Art Loosed*, based on his novel, had been quite successful on DVD. I could hardly believe this, but it got better: Bishop was coming to the Sony offices to meet with Michael for the first time to talk about the movies he wanted to make. As it so happened, my office at the time was right next to Michael's.

I walked over to David, Michael's assistant, that morning and sheepishly asked, "Could you please let me know when Bishop is coming in? I just want to stick my head out of my office so I can see him as he walks in." David was nice enough to indulge me and kindly agreed to let me know. This was all I was hoping for, just a glimpse and maybe a chance to shake the man's hand.

But the Lord had more in mind than I ever could have guessed.

I was in sitting in my office that afternoon, working on various things, when my phone rang. It was David. Bishop was on his way in—and Michael wanted me to join the meeting. "He wants me to do *what?*" I shot back, stunned. After a moment of disbelief, I gathered myself and said, "Of course I'll join, I'll be right down." I was shocked, excited, and nervous all at the same time—but I wasn't even dressed appropriately for a meeting of this magnitude. I was wearing khakis and a button-up shirt, not the shirt and slacks I would have worn had I known in advance. But I had to get over my insecurities about my attire because this was an opportunity I couldn't pass up!

I walked over to the office, and this is the way the seat-ing was set up: Michael and the head of Screen Gems were sitting on one couch, and there was an empty love seat. I sat on one side of it and we all made small talk. Then Bishop arrived. I was in awe. Imagine a lifelong basketball fan about to meet Michael Jordan and you'll have some idea of how momentous and nerve-racking this was for me.

In Bishop walked in a custom-made suit, along with his agent and producing partner, and he sat down right next to me. At this point, I was blown away. What are the odds of this? How am I working in Hollywood and sitting right next to Bishop T.D. Jakes, not in a church service but in a meeting at Sony about the movies we're going to make together? This was nothing but God at work. There was no way that this could have come together on its own.

The meeting went great. An hour later we walked out of the office, exchanged information, shook hands, and Bishop left. I went back into my office, fell into my desk chair, and said, "Lord, this doesn't make any sense. How is it that I'm working with Sony, working in 'the world,' and through that you connect me with one of the most influential people of faith in the country?" I didn't know what would come of our newly formed relationship, but at that moment I didn't care. I felt the same sense of gratitude that I felt after my men's bathroom stall prayer: that feeling you get when you realize that the Creator has just placed his hand on your life.

The next time Bishop was in town, I went to hear him preach, and when I got to the church one of his people led me to my seat. The last time I went to hear him I sat in the nosebleed seats, but this time I was in the front row. The irony was not lost on me; it hit me with (no pun intended) biblical force. God was casting Bishop T.D. Jakes to play a role in my story and vice versa. I also realized that God was making this connection not so I could practice hero worship, but because there was work he needed me to do.

IN THE END, GETTING a movie made is all about casting. No matter how good your screenplay or how hot your director, no one buys a movie ticket to see words on a page or to *ooh* and *ahh* over the camera angles. They buy the ticket to see their favorite movie stars bring the script to life on-screen.

Casting is also the most important step before you go into production. Your cast are the people who will influence your life and career going forward. It includes your coworkers, subordinates, and superiors, the people you work alongside each day. It includes your mentors and teachers both formal and informal. It includes friends who care about and support you through thick and thin. It includes family members, the ones who keep you grounded and are always there for you. And it includes a pastor or spiritual adviser, someone who assists you in dealing with challenges in your faith and in interpreting God's will. You may have graduated at the top of your class or be a hotshot in whatever you do, but there is no business without people. The men and women with whom we sweat, collaborate, counsel, recreate, and pray shape who and what we become.

Who are you casting in your career and what role does each person play? More important, if you lack the cast to bring God's vision for your career into existence, who do you need bring into your life? Without the proper cast in your life and career, it is unlikely that you will ever escape Development. With the proper cast, there is virtually no limit to what you can accomplish.

IN CASTING YOUR STORY, you must assume the role of casting director. Let me explain: in Hollywood, the casting director is the person who finds the actors, from supporting cast to extras, from whom the director will choose the people who will bring the film to life. A great casting director adds value to a production by using his or her contacts to help the director and producer get the actors they want, but also by making bold and innovative casting suggestions.

A Hollywood casting director doesn't sit around the office waiting for the right actors to walk in; he or she makes calls, pounds the pavement, and gets aggressive in finding the best talent. You have to do the same. If you're missing key people from your cast, get out and make contact with them. You can influence the casting decisions by doing something that many people, Christians and non-Christians, have trouble doing: reaching out and meeting important individuals.

God is the Director of your story. But as Casting Director it's your job to gather the people you want to have in your career, although God will make the final call as to which people will play important roles in your life and work. Some of the most important people in my life and career were ones I didn't set out to meet, like Will Smith and JL. God brought me into contact with them. But for the most part, I've taken an assertive, knock-on-any-door approach to meeting the executives and power brokers who have shaped my career to date. Who knows? Maybe I would not be at Sony if I had not gone to the Barack Obama fundraiser so I could make contact with Sony executives. I took the initiative and God did the rest. If I had sat back feeling sorry for myself or waiting for the Lord to bestow blessings on me without me doing my part, I'm sure that things would have ended up differently.

Nothing about being a Christian is passive, and that includes casting your story. Get out and meet the people who can help your career along. Send them e-mails. Call them. Get on their schedules. Make appointments or try to set up a brief call. Refuse to be intimidated by the idea of walking up to someone powerful and influential in your field, extending your hand, and saying, "Hi, my name is ―― and I'm a big fan of your work. Do you have five minutes for me to ask you a few questions?" I have found that almost everyone in a high position enjoys helping those who are trying to climb the ladder. People enjoy sharing their stories and talking with those who value their wisdom.

However, two admonitions. First, do not worry about whether or not the people you are trying to get to know are Christians. Unless you are seeking their help with spiritual matters, it's irrelevant. Just as we don't want other people in our workplace to treat us differently because of our faith, we should not deliberately place ourselves in a spiritual ghetto by getting to know only those who have a similar faith. I have career mentors and advisers who may not be Christians but who are absolutely invaluable to me because of their integrity, what they know, who they are, and how they perform their duties. The wider range of "actors" you cast in your story, the wider range of knowledge you will absorb and the broader your understanding of all kinds of people will become. That's an asset in any business.

Second, do not step out to make appointments and meet possible cast members thinking, "What can this person do for me?" That's a losing approach. All you should be focused on is gaining knowledge that will help you have a clearer understanding of how to navigate your career. You shouldn't go into these conversations thinking, "How can I get them to give me a job?" No one wants to feel that you are spending time with them solely because you want them to give you something more than just their time. Their time is the most valuable thing they could give, so if you are fortunate to get a few minutes with the leaders of your industry, be grateful. There is nothing wrong with asking how to go about getting a job in your particular industry if you are seeking entrance, but leave the rest up to God.

Whenever you venture into the world of networking to establish important relationships, keep service and gratitude foremost in your mind. If you are a person of integrity and genuinely passionate about the path God has you pursuing, you will attract the kind of individuals who will enrich your career.

Here are some tips for getting the most from your networking:

- *KEEP IT ORGANIC.* On short acquaintance, you don't have to hide your faith, but you don't have to advertise it either. Let any personal revelations, including your faith, come out organically. Besides, true faith reveals itself through actions, not words, and true relationships are built out of a natural connection. Just focus on connecting with the people you meet, and let God take care of the rest.

- *DRESS AND ACT APPROPRIATELY.* If everyone in your industry wears suits, wear a suit. If everyone dresses with a more laid-back and casual style, go that way. Again, when people don't know you it's easy for them to get the wrong impression. Stick to the style that is most conducive to the environment you want to work in.

- *REALLY LISTEN.* There are many more talkers in this world than listeners. Have you ever spoken with someone who seemed like they were simply waiting for their turn to start talking? In such a world, a true listener gets noticed. Become one. Listen actively to what people say. Get to understand their point of view rather than debating your own. Ask the occasional intelligent question; otherwise, let people tell their stories. You'll learn a lot.

- *LEAVE THEM WANTING MORE.* When you leave a gathering, you want people saying, "That's too bad, I can't wait to see him again" instead of "Thank goodness that chatterbox is gone." With most encounters, there is a rhythm you can feel. Make contact, listen, say what you have to say, say a sincere thank-you, hand over your business card, and take your leave. If you have made a good impression, you'll come into contact with that person again.

I'VE TOLD YOU THAT you need to take an active, aggressive role in casting your story, but also that God, as Director, will make his own casting decisions, and you must be ready for them. As long as you are doing your part, he will place individuals in your path who can play important roles in bringing you into production.

This happens when someone comes from nowhere to make an impact on our careers. These are people whom we did not pursue and did not know, but who suddenly show up with a job offer, a project, or a piece of advice. When someone appears in our lives bringing us a missing piece of our career puzzle, you can be certain that is God doing his own casting on your behalf. So, while we cannot afford to sit back and wait for God to make the connections between us and the people we need to know, we can be assured that if we are taking the initiative, he will act to facilitate key relationships.

By the same token, it's equally crucial to know who *not* to cast in your career story. Good casting directors know that the wrong person in the wrong role can ruin on-set chemistry and even wreck the film. They are exacting, conducting multiple auditions and callbacks to find just the right talent for the production. If we wish to go into production, we must act with such discretion, knowing the qualities that we do not wish to admit into our careers and the warning signs to look for.

While it is not necessary to limit our professional connections only to Christians, it is important that we learn to recognize people who regard our faith with disdain, intolerance, or a lack of respect. Our faith is who we are; it is the compass that guides our career decisions and modulates our actions. It is wise to avoid (as much as possible) forming close relationships with people who might undermine our faith commitment. With so much at stake, we must avoid people who are negative influences. Those who lie, cheat, steal, or defraud are also not the kind of influences we should permit to stain our careers; "guilt by association" may be unfair, but it can have real career consequences. As much as we can, we should strive to populate our working lives with people who elevate and inspire us spiritually and morally.

CASTING IS ABOUT MORE than people. You and God will also cast *influences* in your career, and this casting demands as much care and sound judgment as casting people. One of the best pieces of career advice I can offer is to avoid casting *money* as the star of your story. It is tempting to make money the alpha and omega of our working lives, because money is such a huge part of every day. We work for a paycheck, and our job is to help the company make money. If a movie that I develop makes a profit for Sony, then my work is considered a success. But as Jesus says, you cannot serve both God and money. Both can exert control over your life, but a love of money will lead you to violate your most cherished ideals to get more of it. If you serve money, you will either fail at serving God or resent him for holding you to principles that limit how much wealth you can acquire.

There is nothing wrong with money in and of itself. Money is a morally, ethically neutral tool that can be used for good or ill, depending on who possesses it. The Bible does not say that money is the root of all evil, but that the *love* of money is. If you love money so that it becomes the primary reason for your work, it cuts at the root of your intention. Money will make you do things you don't want to in order to keep from losing it or to get more of it.

You are in your position for the ultimate purpose of serving God and carrying out his design on earth. If you focus on that service first, money will take care of itself. Your character and commitment to your principles will reveal themselves and make you a person of extraordinary value to others. But if you serve money only, then you will drop your principles in a heartbeat to chase wealth. When we serve money above all other things, we get the corruption that led to the global financial crisis and millions of people losing their jobs and homes. Think about the trillions that taxpayers are ultimately going to pay because of a few people's loss of integrity and obsessive focus on the bottom line.

As a Christian, you are obligated to think beyond that base desire for money. Nothing in the Bible says that God wants us to be poor. The admonishment that it is easier for a camel to pass through the eye of a needle than for a rich man to enter heaven refers to those who make money their God. In the right hands, money can do incredible good. But where should money be in your career pursuit?

I suggest that money be in your mind, but you must see

submission to the will of God as the means by which you will achieve prosperity. Become a person of principle and character, dedication and passion, and there is no doubt that you will be rewarded—not only financially, but with strong relationships, the respect of others, and the knowledge and peace that you are firmly in the center of your purpose. That approach is better both for your bottom line and that of your company. *Sustainable business comes from sustainable people.*

You should also refrain from casting *position* as the lead in your story. Money and position are intertwined; if I come to work every day thinking only about how I can get promoted to a higher position, I am also telling everyone around me that I am in my job primarily to serve only myself. Instead of pursuing position and compensation, we should pursue God's purpose for our work. What does he call us to do in our current position? How can we bless others, inspire those around us to be more courageous and virtuous, or bring more people to the Lord? Those should be the questions we ask most of the time, not "How can I get that promotion and take home a bigger paycheck?"

If I only pursue position, I limit what God can do for me. God is not subject to position; he did not create us so that we could spend all our time chasing after a C-level title at a Fortune 500 firm. He created us to fulfill an important part of his purpose for his people. If we make purpose the star of the show, then we become better at what we are doing, which ultimately improves our position. Purpose is the endgame.

If I make a movie that impacts people in a positive way, then money and position will come to me. If I am pursuing God's purpose, the quality of my work will be better because it serves a higher calling. We all want to be part of a company that values us and compensates us appropriately with money, respect, and status. If I pursue position to the exclusion of all else, it will be obvious to my superiors that I don't really care about the company; I'm there to serve myself. That will impact how they value me, and it will handicap my work. But casting purpose in the lead role in my story allows me to spend all my passion and energy being a good colleague, doing everything I can to make the movies I work on successful, and helping the company win in every way possible. Passion, commitment, and integrity will be noticed—they are the hallmarks of good business and the attributes of someone working with God on the job.

FOCUSING ON YOUR PURPOSE shouldn't make you less astute in business. Part of being a business-savvy Christian is making sure you're being compensated in line with your performance. If there seems to be an imbalance and you are undervalued, pray on it first, then begin resolving this issue with your superiors so that you can continue doing your best work without being distracted by genuine or perceived inequities. Even as you are doing so, remember that character moves mountains. When you are performing your duties with character, it will be a key ingredient in reaching higher plateaus of success. Cast *purpose* as the lead in your movie and you will help God, your Director, produce a masterwork.

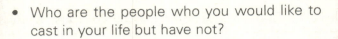

- Who are the people who you would like to cast in your life but have not?

- What are you doing in order to bring those people into your story?

- Have you given money a prominent position in your story? Why?

- How are you pursuing purpose through your work?

- What steps are you taking to ensure that your work is properly valued by your employer?

CHAPTER NINE

GOD'S GREEN LIGHT

Gideon replied, "If now I have found
favor in your eyes, give me a sign
that it is really you talking to me."
—Judges 6:17 NIV

Go! The green light is what every filmmaker, from producer to director to studio executive like me, hopes for.
With a development process that can (and often does) go on
for years, finally getting to that stage where the powers that
be say, "This movie is ready to be made!" is a tremendous
relief and validation. It's the moment when a lot of hard
work pays off—and a new stage of even harder work begins.

With a fortunate minority of projects, the development
process yields a screenplay with strong, compelling charac-

ters, intense action, drama or comedy, and a resolution that ties up all the loose ends, pays off the setups, and leaves the audience satisfied. When the script reaches that point, in most cases we have already attached a marketable star or stars, a great director, put together a budget and production schedule, and run financial models. The entire package comes before the division heads and the chairman of the studio. Only a small percentage of projects that come into development ever reach this point, for any variety of reasons: a flaw in the story or concept that can't be resolved, a missed window of availability with the star we want to make the film with, or a budget impasse with the filmmakers. But regardless of excuses, it's the job of an executive like me to get films made. My bosses expect me to advocate projects that have good commercial prospects and the potential to emerge from development and go into production. If I don't work on films that ultimately get green-lit, then truth be told, I may not have a job for very long.

Studios base their green-light decisions in great part on formulas that take into account the film's genre, the past box office performance of films in the same genre, the time of year for the prospective release, the target audience, and the drawing power of the star. There are many questions that go into evaluating a project before giving it the official green light. Can this movie be successfully filmed for the budget? Can it be finished in time to make the desired release date? What are the potential risks and contingencies? Can it be a profitable film that makes money?

If everything checks out, then the project gets the official nod—the famous "green light." Amen! I've had some exciting green-light experiences since I've been at Sony. Getting the green light for *The Karate Kid* was great, but it wasn't all that surprising because we had a great script, not to mention the tremendous talent involved. When you have power players like those on your film, a green light is a good bet.

An even bigger thrill for me was getting the green light on a film I was developing with Bishop Jakes and Tracey Edmonds, *Jumping the Broom.* This story of a wedding on Martha's Vineyard, where two very different families clash, stars Academy Award nominee Angela Bassett, Paula Patton from the critically acclaimed movie *Precious,* and Laz Alonso from the highest-grossing movie of all time, *Avatar.* It's a relatively low-budget affair compared with the other films I've been blessed to be part of. But it's a special film for me because I worked closely to develop it and because it really represents a new type of faith-based film, one with high production values, quality cast, and top-rated filmmaker. It also explores the virtues of our faith against the backdrop of a fun, commercial movie.

IN YOUR LIFE AND career, God will give you the green light when he decides that you are ready to move beyond development. That means you have become knowledgeable about your profession and how to do your job, matured in managing relationships, persisted in pursuing excellence, and remained steadfast in working according to the principles that make you a Christian. Basically, you've proven yourself and the merits of your character. Now, in God's eyes, you are ready to move to the next level and he can begin using you to have an even stronger impact on the world in his name.

You are ready to move into production. When that occurs, God will put you in the position that you've been working toward or a position that represents a holy hybrid of your desires, proficiencies, and abilities. He will open an important door or place an incredible career-defining opportunity in your path. Now you are ready to produce on another level because you've spent the necessary time in development to prepare yourself. In addition, the results you produce for the Lord are even greater because you've gained a greater ability to influence the people and culture around you in a way that demonstrates his power, mercy, and grace.

For example, if you are an aspiring screenwriter, one of your scripts finally getting made would mean that you go into production. If you are a lawyer at a firm, finally getting that long-awaited promotion means the same thing. If you are a software engineer at an Internet company, going into production might mean that you move from being on a team to running the show for the development of a major new product, something potentially world-changing. Suddenly, your work and decisions have the power to affect millions in spending, thousands of shareholders, and perhaps tens of millions of lives.

Production isn't exclusive to getting a promotion. If you are a teacher, moving into production could mean getting special recognition from your school or an appointment from your district, county, or state. Your position hasn't changed, but you have been granted an opportunity to achieve greater responsibility and influence. You gain the power to alter arguments, support issues, and shape policy. Going into production means you are on a direct path to achieving your purpose.

For a while, I thought that God had put me into production when he led me to Sony after my stint at MGM. Given the circumstances of that transition, I figured "Production will begin my first day at Sony." But I soon learned that while God wanted me to be here, I wasn't done with development, not by a long shot. I'd done some work I was proud of, but I still had so much more to learn from so many great people. That was five years ago and I just now feel I'm entering production. God has put me here to do the greatest job I possibly can and do everything to add value to the company. Writing this book is part of my production. That's a purpose I am fortunate to serve, and I'm still learning every single day how to become the best executive I can as well as the person God wants me to be.

MANAGING OUR CAREERS REPRESENTS a choice. How much time are we going to spend worrying about where we want to be instead of focusing on maximizing where we are? For me, it's an easy answer. We cannot accurately anticipate or control when God sends us into production. There is danger in obsessing so much over the "Why hasn't he?" and the "When will he?" that we miss the "Look what he's bringing me right now!" We can miss the blessing of the moment if we get too frustrated about things beyond our control. In those moments when I'm tempted to do this, I choose to focus on the things I can control: the work I'm doing today.

How can I create value for the company today?

How can I bless those I'm working with today?

How can I improve my story skills so I develop better scripts today?

That is the kind of immediate focus on the job at hand that pays off the long run.

Part of development is allowing God to mature you so that you are well equipped to handle the rigors of production. One of the experiences growing up that helped prepare me was working at church. As a member of my uncle's church, I helped clean up after every service and event. I'd vacuum, sweep the floors, fold up the tables, and take out the trash. This taught me discipline, a strong work ethic, and the importance of making things better not just for myself but also for others. It was great preparation for being in a corporate environment and for doing what I do now.

As Christians, we must be mindful that one of the many rigors of production is increased responsibility. And I'm not talking about on the job (even though that will come too). Production brings an even higher accountability for our faith. In the same way that I am mindful of representing Sony appropriately and understand that my individual actions shoulder a collective corporate responsibility, the same is true for my faith. Since I have made no secret of the fact that I am a Christian, I can do damage to the image and perception of Christianity if my actions at the office do not represent what I profess to believe. So I must do my job in a way that makes God's presence apparent to others. How I conduct myself must tell others everything they need to know about Jesus. As the saying goes, "One bad apple can spoil the bunch." Well, the sincerity of an entire faith can be represented or misrepresented by one individual's conduct.

Our work speaks volumes about whom we serve. If we view our jobs as a form of service to God, we will behave differently. For instance, I will not backstab my colleague if I consider my actions to be representative of my commitment to the Lord. We can't serve God through theft or false witness.

REMEMBER THIS:

When you get the green light and go into Production, you can't abandon the principles, character, and service to God that got you there.

IN NOVEMBER OF 2009, I was included in a feature in *The Hollywood Reporter* called "The Next Gen Class of 2009," about the top Hollywood executives under thirty-five. Well, after I appeared in that issue, someone sent me an e-mail insisting that while he was usually skeptical about Hollywood types who claim to be Christians, he hoped that I would turn out to be different.

There will always be people who are cynical about Hollywood. Hey, most of the news about Hollywood that hits the tabloids is about sex, drug use, high-profile divorces, and gossip of all kinds, so who can blame them? The point is, people in any profession are subject to the labels that others have put on those industries. People in Hollywood are fame-craving fiends. Lawyers are morally bankrupt sharks. Bankers are greedy thieves. Pick a line of work and there's a label for it—and multiply that by two if you're a Christian. Labels are often stereotypes, but grossly overexaggerated and overgeneralized. If God has called you into production in your field, don't worry about the naysayers or the haters. Do not be defined by the labels of your profession. Continue to follow God and let him define you.

Our preconceived notions about our careers can also hinder our progress. I have seen a common issue surface in my interactions with other Christians striving for career success. They self-edit their prospects by presuming that some industries are simply closed to them because they are Christians, even though they might have a tremendous talent or a real passion for that line of work. I see people of faith playing it safe by saying, "That industry would never accept me because of my faith."

How do you know what is acceptable if you haven't stepped out on faith and explored that industry for yourself? I can't even begin to tell you how many people have told me that I shouldn't work in Hollywood. Well-intentioned people—but none of them has ever worked in the business. So while I respect their point of view, I can't let it dictate the direction I go because it's based on fear, not experience. If I had heeded these cautions I wouldn't have the experiences that I'm sharing with you right now. If we remain committed to God, he will guide us where we need to be, but we can't be afraid to experience him for ourselves.

Don't be afraid of overtly declaring your desire to be a success and achieve all the things that come along with success. The whole point of green-lighting a movie for production is that there is a strong belief that the movie can be become a huge success. Do you think God has plans to green-light your career for failure? Not even close. Paul writes, "No eye has seen, no ear has heard, no mind has conceived what God has prepared for those who love him" (1 Corinthians 2:9 NIV). He has a plan to make you successful and you can't fear it; you must get up and pursue it every single day. Go after the promotion—go after the raise. As long as you are not pursuing these things as a means unto themselves but as part of your purpose, go for it and don't be ashamed!

It is tempting to give ourselves an easy excuse not to audaciously pursue the career of our dreams. Perhaps we fear that we would find our faith weakened by the temptations of position and money. Maybe we worry that coworkers would ridicule us or ask questions that we would not know how to answer. In any case, such fears betray us. Whoever said that faith was safe?

Daniel was in the world—he was practically the head of state affairs in Babylon, and it doesn't get more secular than that! Being a Christian isn't about being safe, or being a Christian only in environments where it is comfortable for us. It's about God putting us through the purifying experience of work and struggle in order to perfect our character, integrity, and perspective. Once we have the green light, we will not only have the impact he wants us to have but *remain* the person he has enabled us to become. If you can take that long view, facing a career path where your faith will be challenged ceases to be a trial and becomes a pleasure—a chance to show God's calling on your life and that you are worthy of all he is planning to bestow upon you.

GETTING A MOVIE GREEN-LIT is usually not as simple as developing the script, lining up the right actor and director, and nailing the budget and logistics. The film's timing also needs to be right. It's the same with us. God's timing is everything. Sometimes it's hard to know when he will give us the green light. You might have mastered every aspect of your job and know how everyone else in the company does theirs. You might have produced tremendous value for your employer with creative ideas while adhering to your beliefs. And still, you're not in production. You might pray and ask, "Lord, what else do I have to do?" and receive no answer in return. It can be frustrating.

There can be many reasons why a green light is long in coming, but you should look at them not as roadblocks. They are instead indications that God has more he wants to develop in you. If God felt you were one hundred percent ready for production, he would place an opportunity in your path. A delay may be a note telling you that to reach your peak, you should seek elsewhere by finding a new job or going out on your own.

It is possible that God will give you the green light, but not at your current place of employment or your current stage in life. It's possible that he is calling you to change locations. This happens all the time in the film business. Some projects are green-lit subject to finding a location that is more conducive to the budget and production schedule. Maybe you've maxed out where you are or your current position isn't conducive to your long-term growth. If this is the case, start praying about where God wants you to be. What is the proper location for your production to begin?

In waiting for God's green light, we need not be reduced to passive observers. There are ways to remain active and even accelerate the process of getting the green light. One is to become as savvy in your business as you are in your faith and vice versa. In my experience, people who grow up in a church environment can often be ill-equipped to compete in business. You have to show up and be ready to fight for your future. You have to prepare. You have to strategize. You have to be a competitor. We are sometimes told that we have to be like Jesus, meek and mild. But Jesus is a warrior and a fierce competitor. He's competing for the souls of an entire world and he's determined to win as many as possible. In the Bible, when people were selling at the temple, he turned over the tables. He cursed the fig tree that didn't produce.

That's an aggressive, competitive Lord who is passionate about the business of getting souls for the kingdom. I'll say it again! There is nothing passive about being a Christian!

The Bible is based on conflict and war. We must balance the two halves of ourselves: the spiritual and the assertive. Faith, like business, rewards initiative. You can be competitive about your faith just as you are competitive about your career. You get to the office, do your devotional, get locked in on your purpose for the day, and make it happen. Even if things don't come through, you don't get emotional. You keep the big picture in mind.

The big picture is that God is always in control.

And remember, we must always be mindful that our relationship with him is what's most important. It's very easy to lose sight of this as we are striving to progress. But if you want to move forward on the job, work on your relationship with the Lord. Pray more and study the Word more. You may even need to go to spiritual extremes like fasting in order to gain the power and spiritual purity necessary to persevere and hear God's voice more clearly. You will not be able to endure the rigors of production if you don't prepare yourself spiritually. If you improve your relationship with the Lord, you will have more power, peace, and perspective.

Another effective strategy is establishing a contract with God. One evening after a church service where I spoke, one of the church members came up to me and asked if he could pray for me. I said yes. As he prayed, he told me to write down the twelve things I was trusting God to do in my life, put an X and a line at the end of the list, and sign it. He said, "This will be your contract with God. You do your part and he'll do his." I figured I had nothing to lose, so I did as instructed. To date almost half the things I listed God has done. While at first it seemed strange, I came to realize that it actually wasn't. Most executives have employment contracts, which represent the terms of employment, compensation, and accountability. So why not make a contract with God? In your contract with God, write down the things you want God to do in your career and life, then sign it.

Seriously.

Try it.

This may seem outrageous, but God has commanded us in Hebrews 4:16 to "come boldly before the throne of grace." He wants us to feel empowered when we make requests of him. We serve a God of reciprocation, and as we ask, so shall he provide. The same way a parent provides for his or her child and does what he or she can to help the child find the way to success, joy, and peace. God can do for us all that we ask or think, but we have to ask. Believe me, God will answer.

People think we serve a speculative God, but that's wrong. We serve a definitive God. He doesn't want us to wallow in confusion. When we sign a contract with him, we know it's firm. Doubting that would be like my doubting every pay period whether Sony will take care of my paycheck. You'd think I was crazy. God will always hold up his part of the deal.

The last tactic I suggest in getting your green light (or finding out why God hasn't given it to you yet) is to put yourself in a situation where you have no choice but to see God's will manifest. How desperately do you want God's will in your life? How desperately do you want to operate in your purpose, have peace, and run all the gas that you have in this life out of your tank? If you want those things enough, trust and test God to see where his will is in your career. We all have dreams and desires, but how do we know if they are ours or put there by God to guide us? I knew I had a desire to make movies but I wasn't sure if that desire was mine or his. The only way I could decipher his will for my life was to put myself in situations in which I had no other means of moving forward. When I look at the experiences I've had, they could not have come together in any other way. It took a fierce ambition to learn about God's will for my life to get him to open those doors.

Sometimes we have to take a risk and put ourselves out there for God to give us our green light. When we do so, he gives us a better understanding of who he is and how he is operating in our lives. Once we can get validation and evidence that something is his will, then we have total confidence. When we have confidence that we're on his path, walking in purpose, then forget about it. We can do anything.

BUT WHAT IF WE'VE done everything we set down in our contract with God and the green light just never comes? It's a hard question and a difficult thing to face, but it happens. When it does, it is important to maintain humility before the Lord. We've got to remember that he, not we, knows what waits in the next chapter of our story. This terrible economy afflicting the United States has brought millions, Christians included, to the ends of careers they may have thought would last them the rest of their working lives. But as people of faith we should do our best to rightly regard the end of one career as the beginning of a new path laid out by God, and not despair. Yes, we may struggle financially for a while, but we will find a new purpose in a new career.

When we put ourselves out there with faith, God builds

in us a confidence that we know we are in the right place at the right time. The flip side of this is that we must be willing to listen to the counterpoint: even though we desire it, this career is not what God intends for us. I hear this sort of thing all the time in entertainment. I talk with people who have great passion for being actors, writers, and directors but have been trying for years and never getting anywhere, and it wears on them.

God is not a God of confusion. When we are open, he will guide us. There is nothing so bad as when we are so blind that we cannot see his will. Then he becomes limited in what he can do for us.

If our green light does not come, perhaps it is time to accept the idea that the career we thought was our life's purpose may not be so. When things become stagnant, we have to be open to the idea that God is telling us to take our story in a different direction—to write a new scene. Because whether you get your green light tomorrow in the career you practice today, or five years from now in a line of work you cannot possibly imagine, God has a purpose that will reward you in every way.

- For you, what will going into Production mean?

- What conditions will be in your contract with God?

- Have you been close to green light but not quite gotten there? What were the circumstances and why did it not happen?

- Have you taken risks with your faith?

- What signs have you seen that God wants you in your current career?

- What signs have you seen that say the opposite?

PART TWO
PRODUCTION

CHAPTER TEN

LIGHTS, CAMERA, ACTION!

Our love must not be a thing of words and fine talk.
It must be a thing of action and sincerity.
—1 John 3:18 The Message

Going into Production isn't the end of your journey. It's just the beginning. There is nothing like hearing a director yell "Action!" on the first day of production. In that moment, the story finally comes to life and all the years of development it took to get there seem entirely worth it. However, there is a lot of hard work ahead. People get excited on day one of a movie shoot, but soon everybody realizes that there is a long way to go before the final product is ready for distribution.

Our lives are no different. We can spend years working

our way up the ladder in the roles God has ordained for us—acquiring new skills, developing clear judgment, and so on, waiting for the time when we go into Production. And when that time finally arrives, when God decides that we are ready to apply everything that we learned in Development toward producing results for his plan, it's easy to think, "Whew, I made it!" But Production is only the beginning. We will work harder and longer than ever before during this time, meet challenges that make the challenges of Development seem like child's play, and be asked to learn more in a shorter time.

The product of all that work, time, and intensity will be more than a film, an idea, or a set of skills. The most important result of Production is who you become. The process that starts in Development continues in Production— shaping your character, refining your mind, and testing your faith until you become someone with the influence, standing, and strength to be a beacon of light to Christians and non-Christians alike. *Production is nothing less than the process in which your script is turned into a story that can move hearts by the millions.*

BUT FIRST, THE HARD WORK. My typical day consists of:

- *MEETINGS.* Economist John Kenneth Galbraith famously said in his 1969 book *Ambassador's Journal,* "Meetings are indispensable when you don't want to do anything." That may be true in some organizations, but not in film. Staff meetings or meetings with agents, writers, producers, directors, and actors are where most of my work takes place. During a given day I might have several meetings to discuss the latest version of a script or talk about the endless details that go into putting a film project together. Then there are the conference calls with agents, managers, and various producers to discuss everything from which actors or directors might be interested in a script to which new material is on the horizon. It's all necessary and important. This is a collaborative business built on relationships, and meetings help to foster communication and trust.

- *LUNCHES.* I'll meet with people in the business over a meal to talk about new projects, casting, and any number of other topics. The relaxed setting seems to make everyone more comfortable and lets business get done.

- *READING.* Remember when I said I initially didn't want to be a studio executive because all they did was read scripts? Well, it's true. Almost every weekend is spent poring over scripts and covering them in copious notes to be used in development. The screenplay is where the development process begins, so I'm regularly perusing them, assessing them, and determining which ones have the potential to turn into quality films.

- *MISCELLANEOUS.* Sometimes it's the fun stuff. From time to time I'll have the chance to travel to faraway places like Nova Scotia, London, Paris, Berlin, or Beijing.

Glamorous, right? Well, at times it can be. Yet it's still a job, and no matter how cool any job might appear from the outside, when you're on the inside it's usually a lot of hard work. Even people we all think we'd like to be, from professional athletes to professional musicians, put in grueling hours, months, and years to master their craft and stay at the top of their game. Production doesn't mean you get to sit back, put your feet up on the desk, and rest on your laurels. Quite the contrary.

The same is true when a movie gets the green light and goes into production. What really happens first is that the film goes into *pre*-production, a state that is pure controlled chaos. During pre-production the number of tasks that must be done is endless:

- A production company is created and a production office established.

- There are more script rewrites and the film is storyboarded.

- The rest of the cast is hired, including major supporting actors who might be just as big as the star you've worked so hard to attach.

- The production crew, which can number in the hundreds for major studio pictures, will be hired. This includes the director of photography (or cinematographer), assistant directors, location manager, production designer, composer, and dozens of other positions, each vital to the success of the film.

- Locations are scouted and locked in.

- Permits and insurance are acquired.

- Logistics, which can include everything from accommodations for the cast and crew to shipping equipment and costumes to a location, are handled.

- Finally, when people have moved mountains and everyone is on set, along with cameras, microphones, lights, costumes, props, and about a million miles of cable, production can actually begin when the director says, "Action!"

The amount of work is staggering, most of it done behind the scenes by dedicated people whom the public never sees or hears of but without whom there would be no Hollywood. As soon as the production switch is flipped, the machinery starts moving to turn this idea that's spent so long in development into a real movie.

When we go into production in our careers, the workload is just as demanding. We pass over a threshold into a new realm of responsibility that God has prepared us to fulfill. His expectations of us change dramatically.

In development, our role is largely that of the student. We are expected to soak up knowledge, learn from wise mentors, hone our character, and overcome a certain number of obstacles on the way to greater opportunity.

In production, all that character and knowledge gets put to work. Now we're expected to make things happen in the name of the Lord. As production begins, we must initiate the big ideas we've been developing for years. This is why we went through all those years of development and may have spent some time in Development Hell: God wanted us to refine the talents and obtain the knowledge needed to start developing the purpose he created in us. Think of it this way: Development is about collecting all the building blocks of the person God wishes you to become—strong faith, moral courage, professional expertise, skill with relationships, leadership abilities, a sterling work ethic, and so on. Production is about assembling all those blocks into that person. At its end, you are not the same. *You're better.*

In production, the hours are longer and the pressure is potentially more detrimental. God has allowed us to wander a bit on the road through development to get us to this point and to have us be ready for it. Now he needs us to put in the sweat equity and deliver great works for him. He knows that if we have not taken shortcuts and accepted each stage of development, we're ready to thrive under the pressure.

* * *

IN THE RUSH AND distraction of high-level work, it's not always apparent when we go into production. If you land a huge promotion, that might be a fairly hard-to-miss sign, but not necessarily. What if the Lord plans to put you in production when you master a certain skill, not when you get your own parking space?

Production is about transition, but it's not necessarily about *position*. This is an easy reality to overlook because we are definitely creatures of position. As I've mentioned, it's easy to get caught up in chasing a name on an office door and forget that production is also about *vocation*. In production you cross over an invisible line. On one side, you are still building your skills so you can put the vocation God has given you into action. On the other side is the opportunity to flip the switch on that vocation and start operating more directly in his purpose.

A movie that gets the green light, no matter how promising, has a specific window of time during which it can go into production. If there are too many delays, the project might get derailed. The star might sign onto another movie. A shift in the culture might make the movie irrelevant to its target audience. Or the studio might just lose interest and turn its resources to other films with better odds of being made. Production comes with no guarantees. God will make it clear when you are ready to apply your abilities on a larger stage, but if you are off focus because you're concerned only about the promotion, at some point he might decide you're not ready. The door will close. Focus on who you are; your title will come.

161

* * *

I'VE TOLD YOU THAT when I got the job at Sony, the first picture I worked on was *The Pursuit of Happyness*. The movie was being shot in San Francisco and Oakland. Since I'm from the Bay Area, one weekend while I was home I went to visit the set. When I got to the set, I waited until there was a break in the filming, walked up to Will Smith, and said, "Hey, the dailies look great!"

Will stared for a second and then broke up laughing. Talking about how great the dailies look is just about the most cliché studio executive thing you can possibly say, and Will wasn't about to let me get away with it. He called over to JL, pointed at me, and shouted, "He ain't even been a suit for a week and he's already talking like one!"

Dailies are the best way the filmmakers and the studio can tell how the production is going. They are the film that was shot the day before. It goes to the lab and the lab sends back the footage to watch on DVD or on your computer. You can look at scenes and see if they are being played right, make sure the actors are hitting the comedy beats (if it's a comedy), and so on. If you see something you don't like, you can talk to the filmmakers about redoing it. Dailies are a way to oversee and stay involved in the production when you aren't on set every day. They are also useful for the director and producers because sometimes what feels good on set actually isn't that great once it's shot.

In your life's production, you have dailies you must attend to. How is your devotional time? Are you reading the Word every day? How is your prayer time? Production is a demanding and heady stage of life. You will be pulled in many different directions; few of them will make it easy for you to give your time to the Lord. It's easy to cut out time with the Lord when we're in production; I have been guilty of that from time to time. But when we enter into production is exactly when we need to be even more dutiful in spending time with him.

Time in prayer and reflection is when we get direction about our goals and the things we should be doing to advance his purpose. When our career is booming it can be nearly impossible to find those few minutes to unplug from the world, quiet our minds, and sit in communion with the Father. We have to struggle to find this time. We schedule meetings to help keep our business going—we need to schedule time with God to help keep our lives going in the right direction.

We need time to sit and talk and listen to everything he wants to share with us. Revelations come when we seek his voice. Without that time, it is easy for us to get off track because there are so many distractions. We need his guidance on how to deal with what's coming since we can't see what lies ahead.

Even five minutes a day doing your dailies with the Lord is better than no time at all. Find ways to pull your mind away from work and bring it back to faith. I read Today's Seed, a wonderful online collection of spiritual devotionals that are e-mailed daily. I also get scriptures e-mailed to me from BibleGateway.com. There are many tools you can use to call your mind away from work and back to matters of faith, even in the midst of a busy workday.

Sometimes all it takes is a simple prompt to remind us that we need to connect with God in order to perceive where he is leading us and take steps to follow. His blessing is always ready for us, but we need to see it to reach out and accept it.

At that point, he will give us feedback on the footage that's being shot in our life. He will show us things in our character or our behavior that we need to change or fix. Viewing dailies with God gives us perspective and keeps us focused on the bigger picture so we don't get caught up in the little stuff that takes our production off course.

It takes discipline and self-awareness to remain a truly committed Christian after you go into production. This is the time when it's easy make excuses for slacking off spiritually. There is a temptation to say, "Now that I have this position, I'm sure that God understands I can't give as much time to him as I once did." That is nothing more than a rationalization for apathy. It's a slippery slope from there to saying things like "I'll work just this weekend instead of going to church" or "I can violate this principle because God will really love the result."

Granted, God understands when the work that he has ordained for us demands more of our time and energy. But his understanding does not extend into permission to abandon the devotion that we have given to him. If anything, the fact that he has brought us into this place in our lives signifies that he believes we have the capacity *both* to be more successful in our profession and to retain our spiritual balance. You hear the phrase "work-life balance" a great deal in the business world, but I think the correct phrase really is "work-spirit balance."

Is there an excuse for allowing the time requirements of a more challenging professional life to prohibit us from going to church, maintaining a strong family life, or taking care of body and mind? Hebrews 10:24–25 King James Version reads, "And let us consider one another in order to stir up love and good works, not forsaking the assembling of ourselves together." God knows that as we rise through the ranks and are asked to do more, we will need the support that church provides and the Word that a minister provides. Consistently going to a good Bible-based, Spirit-filled church provides the resources we need to conduct God's business. Attending church regularly helps to replenish those spiritual resources we lose during the week and gives us what we need to excel. I'm mindful that we live in a time when "the church" is changing rapidly. Many services are now being streamed online, which allows a church to reach an audience well beyond those that come to the physical building every week. But even if you get your church online, be consistent and link up with a set of like-minded people who can help keep you focused.

Ultimately, while you should give one hundred percent of yourself to your career pursuit, your career is a vehicle for God to shape you into the person he wants you to be. He wants you to be a balanced person who spends quality time with family, gives to the community, and has a significant life in the church. If you don't belong to a church now that has a purchase on your time and energy, find one and commit to it. It will be a pearl beyond price.

One of my former bosses is an avid cyclist. It helps him balance work and personal fulfillment and enriches his life experience. This is another reason to keep your spiritual discipline and remain balanced: if you make yourself about work 24/7, your experience will be less rich and your performance will suffer. My time away from the movie business, whether it's preaching at various churches, spending time with my family, or traveling, deepens my experience of life. I also learn about people inside and outside of my faith community. I gain knowledge. I will become better at what I do if I keep working on becoming well rounded. God does not want us to pursue career to the exclusion of all else, but to infuse career with blessings from church, family, pastimes, community, and more. If you seek balance, you will produce higher-quality work and be a higher-quality individual.

LET'S TALK ABOUT QUALITY—QUALITY control, to be specific. Even though you might be in a position of greater influence and responsibility, you have to pay even closer attention to every detail of the thing that you're taking through production. You can't delegate and wash your hands of the work. You have to own it. The buck stops with you; that's one of the realities God has prepared you for.

Quality control is critical in making successful movies. Some producers are renowned for their attention to detail and involvement on the set, and I've been blessed to work with some of the best. You can see that in the final product that hits the theaters. A producer who's on the set every day being a partner to the director and helping to craft the vision can drastically improve the overall quality of the film. Sometimes that means attending to the physical look of the picture by making sure the production design is right or working with the director to decide on the best costumes, sets, or lighting. Other times a producer is watching the monitor as a scene is being shot, and after a take he or she goes to the director with his or her thoughts about improving a performance, changing the camera angle, or some other idea. The director won't always use those ideas, but having an experienced pair of eyes on the set is invaluable. It makes moviemaking into a true collaboration, and the quality shows.

God didn't put us into production to get things done fast, but to get them done well. God might keep you in development for ten years until you have just the right mix of skills and intuition to excel in production. Do you really think he will then rush you to distribution? We sometimes get caught up in doing things fast when taking longer and doing superior work is always a better choice.

God is patient.

Production is about trusting your instincts and making the best decisions you can with your experience. You have to rely on your training and trust that God has prepared you to make sound choices and act in the best interest of your company. There will be moments when you're not sure what you're doing, and those are the moments when you have to step back and trust that if God didn't know you were ready, you wouldn't be here—and he has not left you alone. Remember, he has cast your life with the right people to whom you can turn when you need help or guidance.

ON THE WEEKEND *The Karate Kid* opened, I preached a sermon called *This Is It*. The sermon was about our lives and the analogy that I drew was about the late, great Michael Jackson and the *Michael Jackson's This Is It* concert film. The film was put together from the rehearsal footage of

Michael preparing for his last tour, and it is an amazing display of raw talent that many forgot Michael still possessed. But the interesting thing that I noticed was that Michael came to the rehearsals dressed all kinds of ways, mostly in mismatched clothes. Obviously, he was coming only to rehearse so it didn't matter what he wore, because no one would ever see this footage anyway . . . right? But given his unexpected death, what Michael didn't realize was that *the rehearsal* was *the show.*

In our lives, we must come to the same realization. There are no dress rehearsals in life. This is the show. We might think we can get away with showing up at work or church playing the role of a Christian, and as long as our coworkers or church friends buy the image we portray, all is well. We think our great acting skills are buying us time to get ourselves together until the day we'll finally be ready to stop acting the part and start living the part. Yet God is watching and evaluating everything we do. Either we are Christians or we're not. We can't be Christians away from work and then come to work and be something else—and vice versa. The camera is always rolling . . . and God is reviewing what is shot, good or bad. But because he is a merciful God of grace, if we see something in the dailies that isn't right, he will give us an opportunity to make it right. But what if you don't have the chance to make it right?

The first time I preached the *This Is It* message was in November of 2009 at Wings of Love. Most of my family was in attendance, including my grandfather Pops. At the end of the sermon, I asked those to stand who needed forgiveness and wanted to start living the life that God wanted them to live. I also asked them to make a *This Is It* declaration. I could see Pops stand at the back of the church as he made his declaration to God. About two hours later, after we all ate downstairs at the church, Pops got in his car, and as he was driving away from the church, he had a massive heart attack and died.

We all ran over to his car, which had veered over to the side of the road. We were in total shock . . . he was gone.

No words can describe how difficult this loss has been for our family, yet even in the pain, there is peace because I know that when he made his *This Is It* declaration, he got everything right with God. What a blessing that he had the chance to get it right with him before he passed away.

This illuminates the stark truth that unfortunately we don't have the luxury of yelling "Cut!" with our lives like the director does on a movie set. If the director doesn't like the way a shot is working out, he or she can simply do it again. But for us, we don't have the final cut in life. God does. We have to live the way we say we want to live and make sure that the footage that's shot lines up with who God wants us to be. Because God could call "Cut!" on our lives before we're ready, and we may not have time to ask for a reshoot.

ONCE WE ENTER PRODUCTION it becomes *more* important than ever that we demonstrate our faith by our actions, because people are watching. It goes back to the "With great power comes great responsibility" line from *Spider-Man*; when we are in a position to affect how many others perceive Christianity, we have a duty to comport ourselves in a way that reflects well on our church, our faith, and our Lord.

Such choices create value for God, ourselves, our employer, and the community. When we get a promotion or a life-changing opportunity, it's natural to be temporarily dazzled by the higher compensation, the new status, and the contacts—by that overwhelming feeling that finally we've made it. Yet no employer keeps us on the payroll just so we can feel good about ourselves. There is one reason why any employer moves you up the ladder: the powers that be feel that in a higher position you're ready to create greater value for the company.

A film crew works the same way. The lighting techs, grips, designers, and camera operators may love what they do and be excited to be working on a big Hollywood picture, but they are on the set for one reason: to add value to the work that the director and actors are doing. They are there to work efficiently and intelligently, solve problems, and carry out instructions as flawlessly as possible so that the production can run on time and on budget. That is how professionals involved in a movie maintain the integrity and quality of the production. No matter how much they might love their work, if they lose sight of that primary duty, they won't last long on the set.

Quality arises from deliberate action—doing things in the right way with the right goals in mind. These are some of the actions I have found to be beneficial in maintaining a high level of quality in production:

- *TAKE TIME TO GIVE THANKS.* In Colossians 3:17 KJV, the Bible says, "And whatsoever ye do in word or deed, do all in the name of the Lord Jesus, giving thanks to God and the Father by him." No matter how hectic things become we should always pause and take a quiet moment to thank the Lord for bringing us this far. It is a sign of a mature spirit to show gratitude above all things (whether they are good or bad).

- *SURVEY THE LOCATION.* Always take your surroundings into account. How is God moving in your current job? If you are in a new place of responsibility, what new relationships do you need to make? What are the potential pitfalls? How will you handle your faith in this new environment?

- *SET YOUR GOALS.* Know what you want to achieve in your position (at least in the near term) and pray over these goals to make sure they line up with what God's goals are for you in this stage of your life.

- Have you gone into Production yet? How do you know?

- Whom do you know who has gone into Production who has maintained their values?

- Whom do you know who has done the opposite, and what have been the consequences?

- What are your "dailies," your regular devotion to God, and what helps you sustain them with your busy schedule?

- Do you belong to a church? What support does it give you as you pursue your career?

- How do you attend to quality control?

- What are you doing to create value for God and your employer?

CHAPTER ELEVEN

CUTTING IT TOGETHER

*The LORD gives wisdom; from His mouth
come knowledge and understanding. He stores up
sound wisdom for the upright; He is a shield to those
who walk in integrity, guarding the paths of justice,
and He preserves the way of His godly ones.
Then you will discern righteousness and justice
and equity and every good course.*
—Proverbs 2:6–9 NASB

Editing might be the most misunderstood aspect of making a movie. I think it's because of a fundamental misconception that people have about how a film is shot: that it's filmed from beginning to end in chronological order. In reality, movies are shot out of order based on the locations, the availability of actors, and a handful of other reasons. Moving equipment, props, and people around is incredibly costly, so when you have your entire production in one place, you shoot every part of the movie that takes place at that location before you pack up and move. If some scenes at the beginning, middle, and end of your film take place in a small English village, you film everything on that location. That means one day an actor's character might be healthy and happy-go-lucky in a scene from the first act of the picture, and the next he's dying of cancer or shattered by a breakup in Act Three. It's challenging, but that's the way movies are shot.

That's just principal photography, the scenes shot by the director and the main crew. We also have the scenes shot by the second unit, which is headed by a second-unit director. Second-unit footage can be anything from "establishing shots," those exterior shots of a building or mountain intended to establish a place and time, to action sequences. Then there are reshoots, which come when the initial shoot of a scene doesn't go well or the director doesn't like the way it looks, and "pickups," small extra scenes that fill holes the director and editor have spotted in the storytelling, which are usually shot well after principal photography has wrapped. And of course, these days you have plenty of computer-generated (CG) effects shots. A Hollywood film is like a dish made of dozens of ingredients added at different times.

By that analogy, the editor, working with the director, is the chef who has to turn the ingredients into a masterful meal. Editors are the unsung saviors of the movie business. As all this footage from all these sources reaches the editor's office, he or she has to assemble all the pieces in an order that not only makes sense but emphasizes the highs and lows of the story, builds dramatic tension or comedic set pieces, and fits with the desired MPAA rating for the film. An editor might edit a violent scene in a totally different way if the studio is after a PG rating or reedit the same scene if the studio is going after an adult audience and an R rating. Editors can work magic, and the great ones can take the hundreds of scattered scenes, pickups, and CG shots and in a few months produce a box office hit.

Even so, there are always sacrifices for either run time or ratings. Consider Peter Jackson's blockbuster *Lord of the Rings* trilogy. He managed to film all three incredibly complex movies in New Zealand in a year and a half—an amazing accomplishment. But New Line didn't want the films coming in at three hours long, because theater owners wouldn't be able to fit enough showings into a day. So Jackson and his editing team had to make plenty of painful cuts to make the films short enough. The same is true for many classic films, from *The Godfather* to *Apocalypse Now*. That's why, if you want to see the director's complete vision for the story, you have to buy the DVD with the "Director's Cut."

And editing is only one part of post-production. After the film shoot is done, you've also got to create your effects shots. You've got to record and edit your sound effects. You've got to compose and record your score. While this is going on, marketing is ramping up the promotional campaign. Final tweaks to scenes, effects, and sound can continue until a few days before the film is set to debut in theaters. "Post" is a frantic time for a team of behind-the-scenes people. But without them putting all those pieces to-gether the production would never reach distribution and its intended audience.

SINCE I'M DRAWING PARALLELS between each stage of the film development and production process, it's no surprise that I see editing and post-production playing a part in our career progress and our service to God. Editing begins as soon as a movie goes into production. You are constantly "cutting your story together"—pulling the disparate pieces of your career and faith into a coherent narrative that shows you the road ahead of you. Those disparate pieces? How about your superiors, responsibilities, and the expectations of your industry? Add to that your friends, family, and men-tors, then mix in your church, financial pressures, deadlines, and the performance of other people and companies. Some-how, you and God have to collaborate and turn all those moving parts into a career path that makes sense, is consis-tent with your values, and ultimately serves God's design for you in the world.

One of the reasons God often sends us on a convoluted, obstacle-ridden road toward our dreams is that he wants us to develop the judgment, discretion, patience, and diplomacy to cut our story together in an effective way. The reason that you don't see many twenty-five-year-old CEOs of major cor-porations is that it takes years of experience to learn how to weave a vision that moves the company forward.

That's the same reason the best editors are typically the most experienced ones. It takes years of doing and learning from mistakes to juggle the needs of the director, producer, studio, ratings board, and marketing people and still cut a picture that makes sense and entertains. In my job, I'm still learning how to manage directors, producers, writers, and actors and better service the needs of my bosses.

Back in chapter 2 we talked about the Big Idea, having a vision for your career to build on. Well, when you reach Production, guess what? It's vision time again. After an editor gets the footage from a film's production, he or she works from the director's vision and his or her own to transform it into a great film. In Production you must have a fresh vision of what you wish to achieve, a vision that will build on your initial vision. Only with that vision clearly in mind can you cut together the various pieces of your career to produce something inspiring. God will help you clarify that vision through the events and people that he sends your way, but he can't do it without your help.

Let's say that you've spent your years in Development working in construction. You've done your apprenticeships, gotten your contractor's license, mastered various trades, and finally opened your own construction company. You're in Production doing what God intended you to do. But what's your vision? How are you going to take the pieces of your career—your network of contacts, knowledge, finances, opportunities, and so on—and put them together in a way that serves your passions and God's design? This is where vision comes into play. Perhaps you have a passion for ecology, so you orient your company on building green housing. Perhaps you want to help the needy, so you work with churches to help build low-cost housing for the working poor. Those are wonderful purposes, but without a vision to guide you,

you might spend years taking any sort of work that came along, wondering what happened to your passion.

Some ideas for developing your new vision:

- *PRAY.* This should always be your first step. Talk to God. Find out how he wants to refine your Big Idea. Quiet your mind and see what seed he has planted there so you can let it flower.

- *COLLABORATE.* You have coworkers, superiors, and mentors. Ask them what they think your goals should be for the first year in your new position. You'd be surprised at the valuable input you can get from those you work with and how they can help you shape your vision.

- *THINK BEYOND MONEY.* It is very tempting when we ascend to a higher position to dwell on how much money we'll be making. Think instead about what you could do that would make you totally fulfilled and excited each morning when you wake up. What vision will make you fall even more in love with your work?

- *BE OF SERVICE.* This is one of the labels I have stuck to my computer monitor so I'm reminded of it every day. Your first goal should be serving others, because by doing so, you serve God. We don't always realize it, but we're not here to serve ourselves first; we're here to serve others in ways we can't imagine. Always keep that foremost in your mind. I remind myself daily that I am not at Sony just for me. I'm here to help find ways to improve the lives of others, from the producers and directors I work with to the people who handle security on the lot. God will cut together your career so that it serves others first and make you the delivery system of that blessing.

ONE OF THE FIRST friends whom I met when I came to Hollywood was Glendon Palmer. He was an assistant at Handprint Entertainment. He came to Los Angeles in 1993 after he graduated from Northwestern, and we became friends when I started my internship in 1996. Glendon mentored me, introduced me to people in the business, took me to premieres, and basically showed me the ropes. He helped me get established. After JL and Will started Overbrook, he went there as an executive and let me share an office with him, even though I was still a lowly intern.

Well, this business does not insulate us from the happenings of life. Glendon lost his job. His entire goal had been the same as mine: to come to L.A. and produce. He worked hard but was in a tailspin. People he thought were his friends stopped returning his calls. E-mails that once had been quickly answered now waited weeks—even months—for a response. Breakfast, lunch, and dinner meetings were postponed and never rescheduled.

Bad went to worse and he went on unemployment. He hit up every person he knew for an executive job, but struck out. The only job he could get was as a temp on the assembly floor of a nutrition company. It was a humbling, rude awakening to go from executive to temp in less than a year. It appeared that his entire career was going to wind up left on the cutting-room floor.

But what always amazed me was that Glendon, even on the darkest of days, would not throw in the towel. He always had an attitude that said, "I'm not giving up." He was determined to find some way to make it as a producer. He started working on an idea for a wedding movie with his friend, accomplished screenwriter Elizabeth Hunter. Through the hardest of days they worked on the idea and even convinced their mutual friend Arlene Gibbs to write the first draft for free since Elizabeth was busy on various projects. Yet the script had no takers.

Glendon was out of work for almost three years. In the film business being out of work for that long is the equivalent of flatlining on the operating table; your career might as well be pronounced dead. But Glendon didn't quit pounding the pavement. He isn't particularly religious or spiritual, yet he was displaying more faith than many who are. He helped strengthen my faith tremendously because I kept asking myself, "If I was in his shoes, could I keep going?"

I wanted to help but there were no jobs, so the best I could do was pray, and I got my family to pray, too. Finally, Glendon got a job with an independent production company and it looked like he was back on track, but that didn't work out because they wanted to focus more on television than film. But God had a plan. My former boss, Tracey Edmonds, became president of a new company being funded by billionaire Bob Johnson, Our Stories Films. She was looking for a film executive who had relationships and could hit the ground running. Every person she called told her, "Glendon is your man." After several meetings, she called him up and offered him the job. He was finally back in the business for real, at a new company with money and a profile and a chance for him to finally catch that elusive dream: producing a feature film.

In 2007, Our Stories released a movie called *Who's Your Caddy?* Because it was an acquisition, Glendon wasn't involved and didn't get a chance to produce. As I've mentioned, development is tough and takes a long time. So some of the projects he was developing were close to getting made, but the funding fell through. So he had been in the business for years, had never produced a film, and production was nowhere in sight. But God was getting ready to do something.

Bishop T.D. Jakes's film *Not Easily Broken* came out in January 2009 and did well enough at the box office and on DVD that we wanted to produce a follow-up film with Bishop. What we didn't have was an idea that everyone could agree upon. So one day I called Glendon (who always had a lot of ideas on his desk) and said, "What have you got?" He pitched me all the ideas they were developing but none of them seemed right . . . then he pitched me that wedding film idea he'd been working on for years, *Jumping the Broom*. It sounded interesting, so I asked him to send me the script. My initial reaction was that it needed a lot of work; I didn't think it was the film for us or for Bishop Jakes. But after a few months, it occurred to me that it actually had a lot of the elements that fit perfectly with Bishop's brand: it was family oriented, had tremendous heart, and could easily incorporate a faith element.

I called Glendon and asked him if he was opposed to making this a faith-based movie. He hemmed and hawed and hesitated, and then finally said, "Why am I talking myself out of an opportunity? Yes, I bet we could make it work." He spoke to Tracey and Elizabeth. I passed the script around to Bishop and my bosses at Sony. Everyone liked it and we all saw the potential in it. If everyone was on board with making it a faith-based movie, then we would buy the script and develop it. I asked Tracey about it and she was gung ho, so we put *Jumping the Broom* into development with Bishop Jakes, Tracey Edmonds, Curtis Wallace, Elizabeth Hunter, and Glendon producing.

Well, the development process was great, truly one of the best I've had. Rewrites came in and the movie revealed itself; the script was in great shape. We were able to land an excellent first-time director, Salim Akil. But the biggest hurdle was casting. If we couldn't find the right cast, then the movie wouldn't go. We were blessed when Angela Bassett read it and signed on, because that helped us pull the rest of our cast together quickly, which was incredible considering this was not a big-budget film and we weren't paying a great deal. And in the summer of 2010 in Halifax, Nova Scotia, we went into production on the first movie Glendon had produced in seventeen years in Hollywood. When the movie is released nationwide, he'll be able to look at the same movie posters he's stared at every time he goes to the theater and for the first time in his life he'll see one that says "Produced by Glendon Palmer."

It amazes and humbles me that God used me to bring validation to Glendon's lifelong pursuit. Everyone had counted him out, but because he never gave up, I never gave up on him. And not just because he took me under his wing when I first got started, but for a simple reason: He was my friend. Glendon was ready to take advantage of the opportunity when it came along. He had no idea how God would edit his career together in such a profound way. Yet because he did his part by developing the script for *Jumping the Broom* even when he didn't have a job, he gave God valuable footage that he could cut together at the right time.

This is also what I mean by service to others being part of your vision. You're not just pursuing your career because it's going to bless you; God is putting you in that position because he needs you to be a blessing to others. Other people will be blessed if we trust God and let him work through us.

Think about Joseph. God ultimately put him in a position that allowed him to save his family. He became the most powerful man in Egypt next to Pharaoh and had authority over the kingdom, including its food supply. That was cool for Joseph, but when the famine hit and his brothers came looking for food, he was in a position to help them. He was able to achieve the fulfillment of his dream, the one he dreamed long before. God put him in that position not just so he could have stature but so he could help his family survive and redeem their actions toward him with his forgiveness.

ANOTHER INTERESTING FACT ABOUT the editing stage is that God will pull assets from all different areas of your life and career and put them together to create one part of your story. Just as a film editor pulls from principal photography, pickups, and sometimes even stock footage to fit the puzzle pieces into a movie, God will leverage experiences that you might not even remember or think are important and make them make sense for your career.

Take Tracey Edmonds. She gave me my first executive job. But I left her company years ago, so what are the odds that we would get to work together on *Jumping the Broom*? That's how God works. He never forgets the relationship you had fifteen years ago, the class you took, or the invention you wrote down but shoved in the back of a file drawer. Given enough time, he will pull together elements from a dazzling range of your experiences to make up the story of you.

God has put things together for me in the same way he is putting them together for you. He has given us a vast amount of life experience and resources to draw on, like an editor with nine hours of film to cut down to 120 minutes. Since I came from the church, he allowed me to access my faith background to help films like *The Pursuit of Happyness*. He gave me the ability to leverage my music background to get the Alicia Keys song for *Be Cool*. God has helped me put together a career that is dependent on the various experiences I've been blessed to have.

In order for God to bless us in this way, we must let go of our egos and surrender to his will. Even though we are helping write our own script, he will make the final decisions about how our film is cut together. Milos Forman, director of *Amadeus*, said in a BBC interview, "[The] director is a little bit of everything, little bit of the writer, little bit of an actor, little bit of an editor, a little bit of a costume designer.

[A] good director is the director who chooses . . . people who are better than he is. Yes, I can write, but I have to have a writer who is a better writer than I am, I have to have actors who are better actors than I am, I have to have sound engineers who are better sound engineers than I am." God is that Director who is both widely skilled and masterful at his craft.

Of course, it's one thing to know this and another to accept it and trust him completely, especially after you've climbed the corporate ladder and the stakes are higher. But if we allow him, God should always get the Director's Cut of the story. Even though the editor on a film has a great deal of influence over the final cut, in the end the director usually has the final responsibility for what ends up in the theaters. If we are to allow God to place blessings and opportunities in our way, we must have faith that even when we like a scene that's been deleted, his vision is best for our futures.

When we have climbed to a higher position, will we retain the humility necessary to submit to God's edit of our careers even when we don't like what he's left on the cutting-room floor? In James 4:6 New International Version, Scripture reads, "God opposes the proud but shows favor to the humble." But when we move into the corner office or get the big contract, it becomes very easy to start believing that we're all that: *I've come this far, I think I can take it from here, Lord.* We start believing our own press clippings and the next thing we know, "pride comes before a fall" and our brilliant careers are but memories. Such stories are so common in Hollywood that they've become a cliché.

Thus it is even more critical when God blesses us with positions, promotions, and rewards to put our egos in check and remember who got us where we are. It should be a daily practice for us to say to ourselves something like, "I am only in my position through the grace of God, and whatever happens in my career happens for a purpose that I may not see. I trust that it is a purpose that serves my well-being and his glory." The busier and more prosperous we are, the more important it is to continually remind ourselves where we've been. If a reversal occurs in our career we know to accept it as God making an edit to our story, not as something that should cause us to panic or abandon our values. If we listen to God and pay attention to the signs he gives us, we will resist the seduction of the ego.

EDITING AND POST-PRODUCTION ARE also periods of refinement. What you have up to now is really raw material; many directors say that they can't stand seeing the first assembly or "rough cut" of their films, because these cuts are always choppy and disorganized. It's all right; you have to start somewhere. Your career story is no different. When you go into production you face new demands and situations. It's usually chaotic and you're trying to get your bearings. How will your new responsibilities affect your expression of your faith? How will the new people you're working with react to your faith? Early on, it's rough-cut time.

But as you progress, you and God will work collaboratively to polish and refine your story. God will bring people, situations, and opportunities to you and you will gradually figure out how to serve your passion, material needs, lifestyle, and Creator. Don't be afraid to experiment and make the job your own. Editing is a process, not a destination.

What will direct this continual refining process? Notes. Thought you'd left notes behind in Development? Heavens, no. Notes come to the editor throughout the post-production phase—from the director, producer, studio executives, marketing, you name it. Everybody wants to influence the final cut so that it enables them to do their job effectively. The director may want scenes reordered, while marketing may want some swearing cut so the film can land a PG-13 rating. So goes the give-and-take.

Even after we think we've got this success thing all figured out, God will send us notes and expect us to pay attention to them. They may be in the form of people who help us or block us. They might be doors that open or close abruptly. Occasionally, they will be as overt and unmistakable as dreams or signs. God does not play games with subtlety; he wants us to read his notes, but he also wants us to benefit from them. If we are not seeing them, chances are we're choosing not to heed them.

Notes during post-production can be about anything, just as in development. Most often, they will be about actions that help you draw closer to your purpose. Whatever they are, we are wise to pay attention and make the revisions to our story.

When a film finishes photography and gets to the editing stage, it's almost inevitable that it will be completed and released in some form. Too much time and money have gone into taking it this far. But if post-production is contentious or a film just isn't coming together in the editing room, the final product can be drastically less effective and successful than originally hoped. For instance, a movie that turns out to be a disaster in post will still be released in the hopes of recouping some of the investment, but it probably won't be in movie theaters, at least not in the United States. Instead, it will go directly to DVD and maybe to specialty cable channels—not exactly the glorious Hollywood premiere every filmmaker hopes for.

In the end, a good editor is about serving the goals of all the filmmakers to produce something meaningful. Oscar-winning editor Walter Murch, whose films include Sam Mendes's *Jarhead*, once said, "Looking at a first assembly is kind of like looking at an overgrown garden. You can't just wade in with a weed whacker; you don't yet know where the stems of the flowers are." In the context of your story, this means that you don't judge by what you see with your eyes and hear with your ears. You keep service foremost in your mind and have faith that something good will come of the tumult. God is always in the process of weaving order from what appears to be chaos and bringing forth blessings from the most unlikely sources.

Consider again the story of Joseph. He was thrown in jail after being wrongfully accused of adultery. Yet while he was in jail he had enough compassion for his fellow inmates that he helped two of them—the king of Egypt's personal servant (aka the butler) and the king's chief cook (aka the baker)—interpret their dreams. Both interpretations came to pass and, as Joseph predicted, the servant was restored to his position in the palace. However, the servant, who had promised to tell Pharaoh all about Joseph's amazing gift from God when he was released from custody, forgot to do so and Joseph remained imprisoned.

Two long years later, the king was having terrible dreams

and no one in the kingdom could tell him what they meant. It was in this moment that the king's personal servant realized he had broken his promise and remembered how Joseph had helped him. The king summoned Joseph immediately, Joseph interpreted the king's dreams, and the king pardoned Joseph and put him in charge of all of Egypt.

If Joseph hadn't served by selflessly helping his fellow inmates, he would have never gotten out of prison. Even more important, after such a long time and no word from the servant, he probably thought God had forgotten about him. What he couldn't have accounted for was how God would use his kindness to the servant two years prior as a means with which to grant him his freedom. This is how God works: opportunities we think have been forgotten in our past become tools to help cut together the blessings that will save us in our future.

- What pieces of your career do you see coming together to form a coherent map toward your future?

- In what ways has God used you to serve the needs and fulfill the purposes of others?

- How did you end up benefiting from these transactions?

- What notes have you received upon going into Production?

- How do you think God is refining you? In which areas?

CHAPTER TWELVE

MARKETING AND PUBLICITY

*Many a small thing has been
made large by the right kind of advertising.*
—Mark Twain,
A Connecticuit Yankee in King Arthur's Court

After you get a solid cut of your movie, do your test screenings, and make your final changes based on audience feedback, the movie business becomes a marketing and advertising business. For months, your trailer has been playing in theaters, television commercials have been running, posters have gone up at multiplexes, your Web site has been up, and a Facebook page and Twitter following have been growing. You hope that there's buzz and that people are anticipating your movie coming out. Marketing is about communicating something of value to an audience and compelling them to respond. The best marketing is always a two-pronged approach: *here's what we have to offer and you've got to go see it*. That's why, as the release of a major motion picture approaches and everybody gets nervous, the marketing department does a survey called *tracking*.

About three weeks before a movie comes out, Nielsen Research Group is one of the few companies that does tracking surveys that help studios and producers understand what the interest in the movie is and how effective their marketing and publicity have been. If your movie tracks strongly, then you know demand to see it is high and it's likely to open pretty well. If it tracks badly, well . . . tracking time is when the anxiety level for everyone involved in the film is at its peak. Years of work are on the line.

Tracking is done by phone and Internet surveys of about six hundred people divided into four primary quadrants: men over age twenty-five, men under age twenty-five, women over age twenty-five, women under age twenty-five. Pollsters contact people at random and ask them questions that divide their responses into four categories. First, they ask, "What movie are you aware of that's opening on such-and-such weekend?" That's called *Unaided Awareness*, and your movie gets a score for that based on how many people know your film is opening. Then they give you the titles of some films opening soon and ask if you have heard of any of them. That's *Total Awareness*, and you get another score for it.

Next they'll ask, "Are you interested in seeing *Spider-*

Man?" That's *Definite Interest* and the answers produce another score. Finally, the pollster will list films that are opening soon and ask you which you want to see first. That's *First Choice*, and yes, the film gets a fourth score based on your answer to that one. Nielsen combines those four scores and that's what makes up your tracking score. The better your score, the more people know about your movie, like what they have seen so far, and are likely to make the trip to the movie theater on opening weekend to check it out.

The initial tracking for *The Karate Kid* was really good. Not monster-hit good, but very strong, especially with family audiences, which we knew were a strength, and young boys. But as we got closer and closer to our opening day, *The A-Team* started tracking stronger and stronger until by opening weekend we were neck and neck. Why is this a big deal? Because only one film can be number one at the box office on a given weekend, and being number one can make a huge difference in how well your movie does overall. It also increases demand because historically people want to go see the movie that was number one the previous weekend. Being on top becomes a self-fulfilling prophecy. We figured we had a great shot at coming out of the gate at number one, but now we worried that *The A-Team* might knock us off, especially with boys.

Then came Friday, June 11, 2010—opening day. The film debuted in East Coast matinees first. Now, the way we gauge how much a movie should earn on opening day and on its opening weekend is similar to the way a Realtor figures out how much your house should sell for: comps. We find a comparable film with similar audience demographics that came out at the same time of year, and that movie's earnings become the benchmark for our new movie. The entire team, from producers to actors, crossed its fingers and hoped that we had produced a picture that would resonate with people. There wasn't much else we could do. I said a little prayer. Then the first East Coast matinees opened at 9 a.m.

Well, after the 9 a.m. reports came in we started getting excited because we were far ahead of our comp film. By 4 p.m. on the East Coast, the last of the matinees, we had done more than double what *A-Team* had done. Everybody was going crazy; it looked as if we were going to have a major hit on our hands. What made it even more amazing was that box office had been down all year. Any sign of life was great, but for our film to be responsible for it was incredible.

You might be laughing about what happened with me at this point. If you're not, you will be. After you get your matinee numbers, you usually don't hear anything else until about 10 p.m., when the head of worldwide marketing and distribution sends out an e-mail to let everyone know how the film is doing. But this was a Friday. It was the Sabbath! I couldn't check my e-mail or answer the phone, even though everyone I knew in and out of the business would be trying to contact me with news and congratulations (I hoped).

How's that for a plot twist? Here I am finally in the production stage of my career, the place that God has been trying to get me to for more than ten years, ever since I was an assistant, and my commitment to him is going to prevent me from knowing anything about it for twenty-four hours! But that's the way it is, so off went my e-mail. I shut off my BlackBerry and prayed for the best.

That evening, family members kept asking me, "Aren't you concerned?" I said no—what I was most concerned about was that I had to preach the next day at Mt. Rubidoux out in Riverside, sixty miles east of Los Angeles. I'd been attending the church for years and this was the first time I'd been asked to preach there, so I was more nervous about that than I was about how the movie was performing. We had done everything we could to make the movie a success, so no amount of worrying was going to make a difference, but being responsible for someone hearing God through me is a tremendous responsibility that deserved my full attention.

It's amazing how God works things out: one day *The Karate Kid* opens, and the next people are gathering at one of the biggest Adventist churches in the L.A. area to hear me preach at Youth Day.

Finally, the sun went down on Saturday. I turned on my BlackBerry and I thought the thing was going to explode. I had more than one hundred e-mails. I thought there would be at least thirty, but this was insane. We had done close to $19 million on Friday and the projections were that we were going to do about $56 million for the entire opening weekend. That was about $20 million beyond our expectations! Bosses, agents, writers, executives, and friends were all reaching out and offering me congratulations. I was sitting with my family as all this was coming in and the greatest blessing was that I was able to read all this to them. We whooped and hollered, high-fived and hugged. Most of all we thanked God. It was a celebration. At the time I'm writing this, the movie has done more than $355 million worldwide.

Yet, the box office dollars don't tell the whole story. The movie didn't succeed just because it was a remake of a popular title with a built-in audience. (Coincidentally, *The*

A-Team, the movie we opened against, was also based on a popular 1980s property.) We succeeded because millions of people connected to the movie's message of hope, perseverance, and victory. We spent a great deal of time during development and production making sure *The Karate Kid* was about something more than just amazing kung fu filmed on location against some breathtaking scenery. We made sure the movie was built on an emotional and uplifting message. And this makes its success even more fulfilling because it proves that a movie filled with positive themes can be wildly commercial and financially profitable. It is even further confirmation for me that part of my purpose in life is to make and participate in movies that inspire the hearts, minds, and lives of millions.

WITH A FILM, MARKETING and PR encompass everything that a studio does to build a compelling message for the film: create broadcast and online media to promote it, develop visuals like logos, posters, and licensed products, leverage social networking to help spread the word of mouth, put together test screenings that tell us what's working and what's not, and get the film's stars and director talking to Jon Stewart or interviewed on *Entertainment Tonight.*

Typically, this process begins as soon as a picture goes into production. The marketing department of the studio that's distributing the film gets a copy of the script and a roster of the stars and begins brainstorming. Is the film going to have a tagline and what's it going to be? (Example: *Inception* had two, "The Dream Is Real" and "Your Mind Is the Scene of the Crime.") What will the dominant images in our poster and other materials be? What are the demographics of the target audience? How active are they on Twitter or on the Web? When does our first trailer need to hit theaters? There are a thousand questions and a to-do list as long as any for a film's shooting set.

The marketing department will develop a one-sheet, start planning the trailer right down to temporary music, and if appropriate, begin developing ideas for possible commercial tie-ins with companies in fast food, clothing, toys, and more. Marketing packages and positions a film as something its target audience simply *must* see, then leverages the advertising, Internet, and news media to make sure that when the film comes out, everybody knows about it.

In the same way, we market and publicize ourselves. At some point while you're in production, you will reach the point where you begin to have the impact on the world that God intends. This is when you enter the marketing and publicity stage of your career—only God is marketing and promoting who you are becoming: center of influence, source of inspiration, counselor, value creator, and collaborator. You're a finely tuned instrument of the Father, and he's going to let the world know about it.

Marketing and publicity represents one of the most challenging stages for the Christian careerist, because it asks us to walk an exquisitely fine line between letting our actions speak for themselves and blatantly telling other people, "Look how God has rewarded me for being his servant!" I have said there is nothing wrong with ambition, and that's true. The Bible encourages us to aspire to have more and be more. But when ambition gives way to ego, we can find ourselves chasing the approval of others and doing whatever we must to let others validate who we are.

It is critical to get feedback from those we work for and with about how effective we are being at our job. Just because we're being produced by faith doesn't make us "untouchable." We need to know if we're getting the job done. We're no different from anyone else in this regard because we all need validation that we are doing a good job. However, we must not give that validation priority over God's. Positive attention and acclaim can be no different from money or fame. Once they become the drivers of our actions, there's nothing we won't do—no corner we won't cut or principle we won't betray—to get more of them.

But when your faith is producing you, your work and the manner in which you do that work each day say everything about the kind of person you are. It's an unfortunate product of our fame-obsessed age that so many people feel they have to play the "Look at me!" game even if they haven't really accomplished very much. But have you noticed that people who enjoy both success and longevity in any business are the ones who don't spend their spirits on self-promotion? Rather they just pour their hearts and souls into doing scintillating work. From stars like Clint Eastwood and Morgan Freeman to musicians like Bono and R&B legend Ron Isley, every field is full of passion- and talent-driven people who spend decades doing incredible work and inspiring others and let fame and fortune take care of themselves.

When I was still at USC, I was blessed enough to land an interview with music legend Quincy Jones, who lives here in L.A. I went up to his house in the hills and we talked for a while. I asked him during the interview how to become successful and well known. He replied, "You do the thing out of your thing and the people will come to you." Meaning, don't focus on the wrong thing. If you do your work well, and you do it with character and integrity and excellence, the publicity will come. You don't have to go looking for it.

SO IF FAITH DISCOURAGES us from feeding our egos by basking in the credit for what we've done, why do we need marketing and publicity? God will use it in our careers to achieve two ends:

- *Demonstrate the professional and personal value of having faith.*

- *Position us to have maximum impact for his kingdom.*

To make a film successful, every tool in the marketing and PR arsenal is used. You've probably noticed that film studios never rely on a single marketing method to make audiences aware of an upcoming movie. Instead, they use multiple communications channels: trailers, TV commercials, event sponsorships, Web sites, social networks like Facebook and Twitter, press coverage from actor interviews, press tours, posters and billboards, and tie-ins with products from other companies, just to name a few. The thinking behind this is strategic. People are busy, and if they don't get a chance to see your trailer or your television spot, there's a decent chance they'll run into your billboard or come across one of your ads on the Internet. The more ways there are for the public to learn about a film, the better the odds of getting them to come out and see it and turn it into a box office winner.

We are the vehicles through which God markets the value of having faith. But the marketing and publicity are all about showing, not telling. Can you imagine someone closing a big sale or completing a successful project and announcing to everyone, "Did you see how much integrity I had during that last meeting? Wasn't that awesome?" I don't think there's a scenario where that wouldn't be ridiculous, and that's not what God wants us to do. God wants our actions to demonstrate that our faith in him and adherence to his values underlie everything we do and make us better at it.

We do this through our integrity. It's the single most important attribute to possess in business. Much of the financial crisis we are facing today happened because people at various companies had a crisis of integrity. Our faith is actually good for the corporate bottom line and God will use us to show that this is true. As I have discovered in my career, the act of standing for God and doing my best to let him guide my actions can have a profound and moving impact on everything I do and everyone I meet.

The second goal, positioning us for maximum impact, demands action. One of the essential aspects of marketing and publicity is positioning: creating an identity for the film and how we want it to be perceived in the marketplace. The goal is to create and define the film's position before the bloggers, media, and moviegoers do. Positioning in our careers is just as essential because we cannot afford to sit back and let people or circumstances define who we are and what we're capable of. If we do, then we limit our opportunities. For example, I am both black and a Christian. That's great, but does that mean I'm just a black studio executive or a Christian studio executive? If I am positioned solely as a black executive, then I will work primarily on films dealing with predominantly black cast or subject matter. If I'm positioned as a Christian executive, then I can wind up in a similar box.

But if I actively position myself as a studio executive who just happens to be black and a Christian, then I'll be able to work on films that any other studio executive would work on, whether that's action, sci-fi, drama, or films involving the black experience or films dealing with faith. If you don't position yourself as someone who can work on all kinds of projects, you'll get the chance to do only what others think you can do. One of the most challenging aspects of career is to help others see us for who we are and not limit what we can do because of our race, gender, or faith.

How? I try to go after a wide range of scripts and have many kinds of movies in development. This helps define my taste as an executive and expand the box that someone might want to put me in because of my race or faith.

It's also important to have honest conversations with your superiors and not to be afraid of direct communication. We may have a specific career goal in mind or a position that we feel will enable us to be even more productive for the company. But if we don't open a dialogue with our bosses, the opportunities we might be best suited for may never come our way. This is what I love about being at Sony: we have an environment where we can freely communicate and have conversations like this. In your situation, when the opportunity presents itself (i.e., a performance review), be clear about what you want your career to become and how that isn't just good for you but also good for the company. As they say, "Ask for the sale." If there's a higher position available that the Lord has let you know is in tune with his purpose, don't be shy about letting your bosses know you're interested in it. Even if you don't get it this time, you've spoken volumes about your ambition and courage.

TEST SCREENINGS AND TRACKING force the studio and filmmakers to listen to what the audience is saying. After all, no matter how happy the director and producer are with a movie, and no matter how good a job the marketing executives have done, the moviegoing public still has the final word on whether a film hits or misses. Despite the millions spent on trailers, licensing, and advertising, the best marketing is still word of mouth: the millions of tweets, Facebook updates, text messages, e-mails, and mobile phone calls that go out on Friday and Saturday nights telling friends, "This movie is awesome, go see it!" or "It's awful, don't waste your money!" If we listen closely to what the public says, we stand a better chance of being successful.

Sometimes, the feedback from the public is so strong and persuasive that a film may be seriously changed. It's not unheard of for a movie to go to test screening, have audiences hate the ending, and we have to go back and reshoot or recut parts of the movie in order to get an ending that tests well. One recent example was the 2006 picture *The Break-Up*, which starred Jennifer Aniston and Vince Vaughn. One of my best friends cowrote the film. When the movie went to testing, audiences hated the fact that at the end the couple didn't have a shot at getting back together. So Universal sent the cast back to Chicago for a series of reshoots. Like it or not, the audience's opinion counts and we have to pay attention.

In our careers, we face the same situation. When we are deep in production, God will "test screen" our work in order to gauge how closely we are following his path. We need to receive feedback about how others value us as colleagues and constituents. Have we brought greater value to the work of others or enabled them to be blessed in what they do? Such observations can reveal whether or not we are doing our jobs at the level at which they should be done. Feedback will come through performance reviews, contract renewal meetings, and even as informal comments.

In this age of blogging, everyone can be a critic and you can be subjected to withering criticism for the work you do, no matter how good it is or how unqualified the critic may be. This is a difficult but real truth we must face: negative feedback is not easy to handle, no matter how thick-skinned you might believe yourself to be. Even when you are doing God's will and the fruits of your labor are plentiful, that may not stop somebody from saying spiteful things to bring you down. Success also breeds envy and resentment, and when you are doing something you believe in—something that is making a difference in the lives of others—and it comes under attack, it can be tempting to counterattack despite your Christian ideals.

Instead, when you are working in God's purpose for your life and you face unwarranted criticism, remember the example of Jesus. Everywhere he went, for as many people as he healed and as many he inspired to follow his Word, there were almost as many saying ill things about him behind his back.

That's just the nature of standing out.

Yet he never let the negativity get him off of his purpose and we shouldn't either. If you're facing unwarranted criticism, do your best to ignore it and rely on those whom you have cast in your life to help see you through. No matter how tough things would get for Jesus, he had the disciples there with him to keep him encouraged and to help insulate him from those in the crowd who were against him.

On the other hand, sometimes criticism is constructive and justified. On those occasions, a wise person is open-minded and looks to see how he or she can make positive changes. This may involve discovering that you have made mistakes out of pride or lack of faith. Think of constructive or justified criticism as God showing you through the feelings and actions of others where you are off course and how to get back on.

A criticism that I get is that I can be too hard on my assistants, not in terms of yelling or throwing tantrums but it's just that I'm tough on myself and bring a great deal of intensity to my work. I expect the same level of intensity out of those who work for me. My first experience in the business was working for Benny Medina, James Lassiter, and Will Smith. Excellence wasn't a suggestion, it was required. Yet, everyone responds to pressure differently and I'm still working on finding the right balance between having high expectations and being too demanding. I have to be open about my shortcomings so that God can use them as opportunities to fix things that could be a hindrance to my overall success.

Now, consider what happens when you are right on track with God's plan for your career. When you test screen a movie that has been written and directed with vision and skill, you will get the same feeling that we get when we screen a movie that is hitting all the right character notes, the right highs and lows in the story. When that happens, there's energy to the audience that's palpable. You can feel how much the story has drawn them in and captivated them. Two hours in the theater seem to fly by in minutes, leaving everyone wanting more.

God reveals positive reactions in his own ways. Look around. Listen to others. Do you receive opportunities to be involved in work that would normally be beyond someone of your experience? Does morale improve when you are leading a project? These are all signs that you are allowing God to market you in the right way. You are sending the right message and representing God in the way that pleases him greatly. This isn't a time to become overconfident or assume your odyssey is over, however. Say a silent prayer of thanks, remind yourself that credit belongs to the Lord, and get back to what you do well.

- What does your work say about who you have become?

- How are you marketing Christianity to other people?

- How are you communicating what you want and what you can do to your superiors?

- How have you fallen prey to the desire to pursue credit for your achievements?

- How have you put yourself into test screening?

- What are you doing to invite the feedback of others?

CHAPTER THIRTEEN

GOD'S DISTRIBUTION PLAN

The man who abides in the will of God
wills nothing else than what God is, and what He wills.
—Meister Eckhart, Sermon IV, *True Hearing*

Distribution is the point at which a new film goes into theaters and the public gets to decide for themselves if all the hype leading up to the release was worth it. It is one of the most essential, powerful aspects of the movie business, despite being one that the public knows almost nothing about. No matter how great the film or how big its stars, you still need a plan—created by an experienced distribution executive—to get it into the right theaters. If your film doesn't have strong and well-planned distribution, all those years in development and then all the time spent in production could be in vain: you have a finished product but no means for anyone to see it.

There are many types of distribution—direct to DVD, pay-TV, and online to name a few—but the crown jewel of distribution is theatrical distribution. This is the most coveted because it gets the movie to the widest audience possible. As you can imagine, it's an exciting but nerve-racking time when a major motion picture finally goes into theaters to face the judgment of the public. Years of labor come down to 120 minutes in a darkened theater, after which audiences emerge to tell their friends and family whether your work is worth seeing or not. There is a great amount at stake for thousands of professionals, from actors to executives to directors to producers, as a film releases. When the reviews are good and the box office numbers strong, there's a huge, collective exhale from everyone involved in the project. It's validating to have one's work received successfully.

Distribution happens like this: The studio's head of distribution identifies the ideal number and location of theaters for the movie based on what the movie is, the time of year, and who the movie plays to, like preteens or families with kids. Then the department creates a plan that's geared toward maximizing the audience for the movie, which maximizes the movie's value to the studio. For example, a faith-based movie might get released in seven hundred to one thousand theaters in certain markets, because these markets have historically proven to be the most receptive to this kind of movie, whereas a sci-fi film might get released in twenty-five hundred to three thousand theaters.

You can get some conflict when the filmmakers want to have the picture on more screens but the studio is reluctant. Getting it to each of those additional screens comes with costs, such as creating additional prints. But let's say you release a film on three thousand screens but it does well on only one thousand. The value of the picture isn't being maximized. Being in only the strongest one thousand theaters enables a movie to play well in the right markets where the audience already has an appetite for it. Distribution is about maximizing the value of what you have produced.

When a film is released, you see the impact right away. Reviews come out in newspapers and magazines and on radio, television, and the Internet. Word of mouth begins to spread and you quickly get an idea of what the "buzz" is for a film, including whether it's a possible Oscar contender. The box office grosses are public, with magazines and Web sites publishing weekly updates of the top ten grossing films and the money they've taken in. In the movie business, the chief indicator of that impact is the performance at the box office; everything in distribution is geared toward making it as big as possible.

God has a distribution plan already laid out for you at this very second. He has evaluated who he's made you to be, assessed your work, figured out where and how you can have the maximum impact possible, and devised a plan to distribute what you have to offer to the world. Just as a studio has a strategy for getting its movies into certain theaters, God has a plan to distribute your impact farther and wider than you may believe possible to the audience that needs it most.

* * *

ALTHOUGH WE MAY KNOW this intellectually, it is easy to wonder, "How do you intend to use me, Lord? What's your plan?" I struggle with this impulse all the time. I believe that I am in Production, yet I'm not exactly sure how God's distribution plan is going to play out. I know he wants to use me in this world, and that all the time and work I have invested are to shape me to become better at what I do so that I can inspire as many people as possible. I know that God wants me to be in the movie industry and in ministry. But sometimes it's hard to see how it's all going to play out.

Since you are reading this book, there is something in you that hungers for success. Not the superficial success that hoards money and craves notoriety as though they were ends in themselves, but success as we have defined it: validation of who you are, faith in your competence, and security in your calling. Through God, you are operating in a position where you're able to achieve all of this. Distribution is ultimately about finding your place in the world—finding out what your success means beyond what it means for you personally. How can you impact your humanity for good? How can you change things for the better? How can you help win souls for the Lord through your example? Distribution is how you find the answers.

Everything you have done to this point is preparing you to operate in that place and to have an extraordinary impact. Like an experienced head of distribution at a film studio, God will implement the plan that he knows works best, even if we don't understand it. However, we can affect what type of distribution we ultimately get. As always, we are collaborators with God.

As he always does, God gives us the freedom to choose what we will do with the distribution plan he gives us. We can choose to trust God and follow the path he has laid out or we can, as I've mentioned, decide that we know a better way. For an example, look at Samson. God created him with divine strength like no human before him—he was like a superhero. Yet he put down his faith in favor of ego and pride and he let Delilah and the Philistines get the best of him. Because he chose to leave himself vulnerable, they stripped him of the very purpose and power God had created in him.

God is so merciful that he gave Samson an opportunity to get his strength back, destroy the Philistines, and redeem himself, but not only did it cost him his vision, it also cost him his life. Do you think it was God's original plan for Samson that he would die blind and broken in a pile of concrete and rubble? I rather think God would have distributed Samson far and wide to protect his people and to right wrongs. The blessing was that God still distributed Samson to achieve his purpose, but because Samson chose to forsake God, he paid a cost far greater than he could have ever envisioned. I believe God had an entirely different distribution plan for Samson, one that wouldn't have cost him his life.

IN 1 CHRONICLES 28:20 NIV it reads, "David also said to Solomon his son, 'Be strong and courageous, and do the work. Do not be afraid or discouraged, for the Lord God, my God, is with you. He will not fail you or forsake you until all the work for the service of the temple of the Lord is finished.' "

When we don't go into distribution despite believing that we are truly ready, it is usually because distribution isn't just about being ready, it's also about being in the proper season. There are times when movies are ready for release but we hold on to them until the right season of the year comes around to distribute them. Nothing is worse than putting out a good movie at the wrong time of year. Imagine distributing a Christmas-themed movie on Memorial Day weekend. The movie would almost certainly bomb.

When we're ready for God to put us out there and he's not doing it, it can be a deeply frustrating time. It's no different in the movie business; sometimes a film just doesn't come together despite the efforts of a lot of talented people. Something is missing. The demand is poor. The prospects for success seem dim. At times like these we can lose ourselves in uncertainty. We've done the work, we know we have grown, we feel in touch with God's intention, and yet . . . nothing happens. Why? Is it that we haven't arrived at the place we want to be? Why not? What is God waiting for?

It's easy to become impatient and even angry with God because we think he is holding us back. But he is an experienced distributor. If we stay true to him, his distribution plan will commence when the season is right.

God says: "I've got this. I already have a plan for the movie I'm making in you. I have a plan for your next project, for who's going to need you the most. Just do what you do. I've got your back." Even if you think you missed out on the ideal project, it probably wasn't right for you and God knew it. As long as you resist the temptation to go rogue and put your judgment before the Lord's, distribution will come in the exact way he has intended.

Waiting for God's distribution plan to take effect is a rigorous test of our trust in him. We must put events into the context of our life and career. What has happened in the past? How did God guide us to our career? Did he fulfill the trust we had in him before? Why should this time be any different? The alternative is to think we know better than God and start following our own path rather than his.

For example, what if God's plan was to release you theatrically, but you resist his will, so now the best he can do is implement Plan B, which is direct-to-DVD release? Make no mistake, God always has multiple plans in place for your future. Plan A is his highest purpose for you, but you must be firm in your faith in order to follow God's signs leading you to that path. If you fail to pay attention to his Word or put your will before his, you may miss that higher calling and you will have to settle for Plan B. If you continue to ignore his voice, then Plan C may be your only option, leaving you far from where you had hoped you would be once upon a time.

When the head of distribution for a movie studio chooses theaters for a release, that choice is based on years of knowledge of those theaters and how they work. He might place a film in a certain Los Angeles cinema but not in another because he knows the theater owner turns his movies over too quickly. Those decisions are based on long vision and understanding. God has the long vision and understanding of how we will be most successful, and he has already gone before us and identified which projects will be best for us in his distribution plan. We can't get upset when we don't get certain opportunities when we think we should or because they appear right for us. God really does know best.

If you're not sure and need reassurance, ask. A distribution plan isn't a "Shut up and do it" deal. We can have a dialogue with the Creator about his intentions. In a studio setting, the head of distribution may present the distribution plan, and the filmmakers will say, "But we really wanted it in these theaters." A dialogue will start. The filmmakers may not get everything they want, but there can be compromises and they will learn about the reasons for the distribution plan.

When you feel that God is doing something that you don't understand, open a dialogue with him. Ask him what's up. You can't know if something that comes your way is part of God's intention unless you ask. God welcomes our questions; he doesn't want us to be passive. Moses was famous for his back-and-forth dialogue with God. When Paul was converted, he had a dialogue with the Lord. Even Jesus questioned the Father in the garden of Gethsemane, when he asked that the cup pass from him. But in the end, Jesus came to know that God's distribution plan was the right plan, and he submitted to his Father's will.

Distribution demands that we surrender control. We are open to the world's judgment; there is nowhere to hide. Just as we must trust God, we must learn to trust the gifts that he has placed within us. If we cannot, we second-guess our decisions and we might even find excuses to dodge distribution. *I'm not ready yet. I don't have what it takes.* We lose faith in ourselves, and isn't that really losing faith in God?

*　*　*

ONE OF THE MOST overlooked aspects of distribution is that it's not about us. That's an understandable mistake; we're focused on our own fortunes and how God's plan for us will take shape. But when you start to understand how God operates, it becomes clear that he will also implement another kind of distribution plan: a plan to distribute blessings to others through our talents and actions.

I'll give you a wonderful Hollywood example. You probably know Tyler Perry. He's an actor, director, screenwriter, producer, and all-around hit machine who, in about six years, has become one of the most powerful people in Hollywood. His movies like *Diary of a Mad Black Woman, Madea Goes to Jail,* and *Why Did I Get Married*, along with *Tyler Perry's House of Payne* and *Meet the Browns* TV series, have generated close to one billion dollars in revenue. I was fortunate to have the chance to fly out to Atlanta to meet with him at his own Tyler Perry Studios.

It was absolutely amazing. Tyler has literally built Hollywood outside of Hollywood. He has his own studio on thirty acres of land: soundstages, back lot, office space, commissary, you name it. He has plans to expand to sixty acres. It's an incredible operation that lets him work in Atlanta, close to a rich talent pool and a strong faith community, for a lot less overhead than he would have paid in Los Angeles. But what was most impressive was the idea that hundreds of people who work at TPS get up and go to work and have employment because Tyler is operating in his purpose. What a revelation!

Distribution isn't just about our production. Sometimes

God will use us as a distribution center for things that other people need. He used Tyler Perry to distribute jobs to hundreds and to enable them in turn to pursue their own development and production. In return, they all help Tyler continue to build his influence in Hollywood and the world beyond Hollywood. It's a virtuous cycle. This is how God works: he develops you through challenging times, takes you into production, and when you become accomplished and wise enough to be a center of influence, he sends you out to bring knowledge or opportunity to others of his children. You can become a distributor only when you are ready for distribution yourself.

God's distribution plan puts us in position so that others can be blessed. I'm sure Tyler couldn't have accounted for how massive God's distribution plan is for his life, and neither can we. Tyler's experience is a wonderful example of how fast you can advance in your career if you fully surrender yourself to God's distribution plan. Not that long ago, this brilliant creative and business talent was *homeless and living out of his car.*

Yet God laid out a path for him to follow: building an empire of movies based on his stage plays, which centered on Christian themes of family, faith, forgiveness, and self-worth while exposing difficult topics like child abuse. Instead of resisting God's mandate in favor of his own ideas, Tyler fully embraced it, turning out one profitable movie after another at an incredible pace. The speed of his rise may mystify some people, but it doesn't surprise me; I know that's God at work. It's a perfect case study of what a talented person can do when he faithfully follows where God leads and seizes each opportunity with vigor.

Another terrific example of this principle in action is the rise of Joel Osteen, pastor of Lakewood Church, the largest church in America. I got to know Joel a few years back and we have remained close ever since. His story is an example of how God can bring us into distribution quickly and powerfully, and how if we fully embrace the experience and leverage all the opportunities it provides, we can achieve incredible things for ourselves and others.

Joel's father, John Osteen, founded Lakewood Church in Houston, Texas, back in 1959. After working with his father for seventeen years and producing the church's television program, Joel took the reins of Lakewood in 1999. At that point, he had preached only once, the week before his father passed away. Talk about going into distribution under pressure! But Joel proved he was up to the challenge, and his life-affirming preaching style helped Lakewood grow to become the largest evangelical church in the nation.

In a relatively brief time, Joel has become one of the most influential figures in Christian culture. As you probably know, he has written multiple mega-bestselling books including *Your Best Life Now* and *It's Your Time*, which have introduced millions to the ways in which God can bless their lives and careers if they trust him. He has also built a broadcast ministry that reaches millions of weekly viewers in over one hundred countries and regularly produces huge revivals at stadiums and arenas around the United States. Joel is producing incredible results in God's name, but it's never been just about him. He is distributing blessings to millions through the jobs he has created, the uplifting power of his books and other media, and the example of his life.

Then there's Reggie Andrews, a music teacher at Locke High School in Los Angeles. Teachers have many opportunities to distribute wisdom and hope, and Reggie is no exception. One of his students was a young man named Tyrese Gibson, who grew up in gang-ridden Watts and for whom Reggie became a mentor and the father he never had. Reggie encouraged Tyrese to develop his beautiful singing voice, and this led to commercials, modeling, a hit R&B album, and breakthrough roles in John Singleton's movies *Baby Boy* and *2 Fast 2 Furious*. It's reasonable to assume that if Reggie Andrews had not been around to distribute God's love and guidance, the world might not have been blessed by Tyrese Gibson. There are many ways to go into distribution and impact the world in a positive way.

WITH MOVIE STUDIOS, NOTHING is left to chance. There's simply too much money at stake. So each studio has a long-term release schedule that lays out the dates its films will hit theaters more than a year into the future, sometimes longer. Sony has a slate of upcoming films that usually extends out about two years. This is done because part of successful distribution is taking into account not only the time of the year a film is released (action pictures in summer, family films around Christmas) but also the competition. No studio wants its action picture targeting twenty-five-and-under males to debut on the same weekend as *Iron Man 3*. It would be box office suicide.

God has his own release schedule and we all have a place on it. It's based on a huge range of factors: the knowledge we've gained, the wisdom we've developed, our spiritual dis-cipline, our current position, the people in place in our lives, what's going on in our profession, the world, and beyond. None of us can begin to fathom the complexity of God's release plan, but he has taken every facet of our lives and careers into account in creating our strategy. Like the release plan at a studio, the purpose of God's plan is to release us for distribution at a time and under circumstances that will maximize our value to ourselves, others, and God.

So while you might have in mind that the perfect time for you to go into distribution would be right after you make manager at your company, God may have another schedule in mind. He may see that when you make manager, you will still be making personal connections, or that economic con-ditions will not permit the kind of calculated risk at which you excel. So he will bide his time and force you to bide yours; if you stay committed to him then you cannot go into distribution without his approval, even though you might think you are already there.

When the release schedule is in place, God will put you into distribution and you will know it. Events will transpire that let you know you are now at a stage of your career where you have the power to make things happen. This is the time for which God has held you back, waiting until your release can have the greatest possible impact for the kingdom.

Consider the epic story of Moses. Like Joseph, he was a stranger in a strange land: the adopted son of the Egyptian royal family and brother to Ramses the Great—but hiding his Hebrew heritage. God placed him in this extraordinary position for what reason? To enjoy the riches of a pagan kingdom? To preach the Word? No. God set the events of Moses's life in motion because he needed a man of exceptional, unsurpassed strength, conviction, and faith to lead his children out of slavery and to help found the state of Israel.

To that end, God did not distribute Moses to lead an armed revolt from within Pharaoh's palace, nor to overthrow the government from within. Instead, after Moses killed an Egyptian who was beating a Hebrew slave, he fled and became a humble shepherd in Midian. There he refined his character and his faith, coming into contact with God and receiving his command to return to Egypt and lead his people from bondage. In this way, with God's limitless power behind him, Moses was released into distribution as the herald of freedom and the leader of his people.

God's release schedule is in place, waiting for the right time and setting for you to go into distribution. Can you embrace your circumstances with the same faith and fervor that Joseph did? If you can, then your success story may also prove to be one for the ages.

- Do you believe you have reached distribution?

- If not, what do you believe is preventing you from going into distribution?

- What does your impact on the world say about how well you have served God?

- Have you been in dialogue with the Lord? What form did it take and what was the outcome?

- How has God used you to distribute blessings to others?

- What do you want your impact on others to be?

CHAPTER FOURTEEN

YOU, THE SEQUEL

His master replied,
"Well done, good and faithful servant!
You have been faithful with a few things;
I will put you in charge of many things.
Come and share your master's happiness!"
—Matthew 25:21 NIV

In Hollywood, it's all about the sequel. Nothing makes a studio happier than when we can make another installment of a successful film. Many of the movies that are released each year are sequels to previously successful films. Some are the latest installments of highly profitable franchises such as the *Twilight* movies. In film, a sequel takes characters and a world that we love and are familiar with—

223

from *Transformers* to *Men in Black*—and introduces new situations and new conflicts. Audiences turn up in droves to see how their favorite characters will make it out of their new predicaments.

Sequels in movies and in life's story usually get made for a very simple reason: because the first story was such an incredible success. Studios get a lot of grief for producing sequels year after year, but the reason we do it is that the audience has said that they love these characters and their world. They hunger for more. So we meet that demand by taking those familiar characters and stretching them, putting them in situations that are outside both their experience and comfort level. A sequel continues the hero's journey, and it doesn't hurt that they are a reliable source of profit as well. The challenge in a sequel comes in continuing to be creative and find new ways to connect with the audience while remaining loyal to the elements that made the first picture a winner at the box office.

Bishop Jakes once said that we go from zero to ten in our endeavors, and once we max out what we can do on one level, we start over at zero again but on the next level, taking with us whatever we learned during the previous one. Life is a continual process of starting over, becoming better and wiser. The nature of a journey is that we move for a while, stop, gather ourselves, reflect upon the lessons we have learned along the way, and then step back onto a new path with new hope and a new destination. That is the next step in your journey through your career: the sequel.

When God calls you to make your sequel, he is giving you the opportunity to use your abilities in a new way and go back into Production with something else. As Jesus said in the Parable of the Talents, "Well done, good and faithful servant! You have been faithful with a few things; I will put you in charge of many things. Come and share your master's happiness!" God is giving you a new opportunity to use your talents, to repackage your purpose and enjoy life on a whole new level. Most important, he is giving you his seal of approval. A sequel can be a sign of tremendous success on your part. You have performed so well in faith and commitment to God that he wants to take you on a new journey and tell a new story through you. With each completed production, we satisfy a small part of God's great design. Then he will call us to begin anew.

However, sequels are not always the result of incredible success. It's more complicated than that. The first Austin Powers movie, *Austin Powers: International Man of Mystery*, was not a smash hit. It did only about $50 million in box office domestically. But New Line Pictures believed in the character and the vision of director Jay Roach and star Mike Myers. They also liked that the film did well in DVD sales. So they green-lit a sequel, which earned more than four times as much as the first movie. In fact, both Austin Powers sequels earned more than $200 million domestically. That's an example of a sequel arising not from exceptional success but from the belief that there was something special about the work.

In reality, there are four kinds of sequels God can send you into:

- You produce a spectacular success and the Lord immediately turns you around into a new project, building on that success.

- You produce a great success, but God directs you back into Development to master some aspect of yourself that remains underdeveloped. This usually involves getting out of your comfort zone and taking on an unfamiliar challenge.

- You reach a point in your career where you become bored or dissatisfied with your work and leave to begin a new career that speaks to your passions.

- You lose your job and are unemployed, seeking answers during a difficult and disorienting time.

Each of these sequel scenarios has its own blessings and challenges, though some can be difficult to perceive at first. In the end, all require trust in the Lord and his purpose: to bring you back into production in a manner that allows you to have an even greater result than you had the last time. God will always have a new story in mind for you; the trick is to be patient and trust that it will come when you and the world are ready for it.

THE MOST SATISFYING SCENARIO has to be when God sees our work in production, decides it is good, and sends us right back to work for him in a new project. God has us develop our sequel because he loves what we have become in our careers and he has further plans for us. How phenomenal does it feel to know that the Father has seen our development and is impressed enough to ask us to take what we have done and repeat it on an even higher level? This is a time to rejoice and be glad! God is giving you an assessment and you're getting nothing but rave reviews. You have performed so well in his name that he is going to give you an even greater goal in his service.

However, just because we have ventured successfully through production doesn't mean the return journey will be any easier than the first trip. God sends us to make a sequel because he wishes to use us in new ways for his purpose, but he also has things to teach us. They won't always be easy lessons.

Expectations will inevitably be higher when you have achieved one success in your career. When a film makes hundreds of millions of dollars, the pressure is on for the sequel to exceed that box office performance. Everyone wants to know if you can deliver excellence once again. God will also send you to your sequel with higher expectations. He knows that you have gained skill and understanding and wants you to get into production a second time with even greater results. Yet these high expectations are not a burden; they are a gift. God believes you're capable of miracles. He sees the potential in you to do so much more, and if you remain faithful he will bless you with everything you need to reach untold heights in your career.

You inspired one hundred people before? Great. Let's inspire one hundred thousand next time.

Your vision improved life for the people in one neighborhood? Okay, let's change the lives for the people in an entire city.

That's how this sequel works: God believes you have

what it takes to seize on whatever made your production a smash hit and take it to the next level, whether it's a new product launch or opening another location of your small business.

With each film I work on, I ask, "What's it going to take for me to do it again, only better?" I want to keep building my skill set and take a leap of faith into new tasks and new ideas. A successful sequel can't just be a rehash. If you want a real triumph, then you can't repeat what you did before. Instead, you take the elements that worked before and add new tension, action, setup, and payoff. You tell a story that's familiar but different and take your audience on a new journey.

It's vital to stay grounded and keep God front and center as you begin your next project. Even as I go ahead with other projects and try to make progress in my career, I remind myself every day to be humble and receptive to everything God brings my way. Just because I've worked on successful films doesn't mean I can let up even a little bit in my commitment to him—to working with integrity, faith, and fairness. The minute I let any amount of success go to my head is the moment any future plans God may have for a sequel could get scrapped.

When we taste success, we need to come back the next time even more steadfast in our commitment to the principles and values that make us Christians. When we surrender them in order to chase after another success for its own sake, we make it more difficult for God to bless us. To repeat our good works means bringing God to the table. With him even more involved, we can meet those loftier expectations. Deepen your commitment to the standards of behavior that defined your first journey to Production, and you will create another hit in your life.

I'M BEST WHEN I go all in on a movie. If someone gives me a responsibility, I take it literally and very seriously. It becomes my life. *Obsessive* is a strong word, but I have to be honest—sometimes it applies. I put everything I have into a project, into the details and the minutiae, until I get it done right.

But I've learned that you can be too hands-on. In this business, you also have to stand back and allow people to play their roles. You can't micromanage or you'll choke your movie to death. I believe there is an intrinsic benefit to giving yourself over to your work so completely, but I've also learned that what's an asset in some circumstances can be a detriment in others.

I'm humbled and grateful that over time, God has shown me my weaknesses. One of the gifts of Development and Production is self-knowledge, and it's priceless. Through the process of navigating the ups and downs of our careers, we will discover many truths about ourselves—our strengths and weaknesses, talents and passions. It's a marvelous blessing from God to have the privilege to become more self-aware.

In writing the second kind of sequel, you're going to get to know yourself and God even better. Just as I have, you will become acutely aware of your faults and weaknesses and be given opportunities to turn them into strengths. In this alternative sequel, you may have performed exceptionally in Production, but God doesn't want you to turn right around and start something in the same vein. He either sees qualities in you that could still benefit from Development or he needs you to bring your abilities to an area that better serves his purpose. Either way, in this sequel he will send you back into Development to face new challenges. Be glad; he's giving you the chance to expand your capacity to produce and to hone your character even more!

In this sequel God will shape events so that we exit the comfortable envelope created by our prior success. He often does this because despite the fact that we performed so well in one area of our work, there is another where our talents are more badly needed. Companies make this sort of decision frequently: taking a skilled and gifted executive out of a department where he or she is a proven winner and tasking him or her with turning around a troubled division, territory, or subsidiary. Even though such moves can be frustrating when all you'd like to do is sit back for a while and enjoy the fruits of your labors, they also constitute deep praise. No company chooses just anyone to revive a stalled project or resurrect a dying division; it takes someone of great skill, character, and determination.

Career, among other things, is a mirror that reveals who we are becoming. God wants us to discover who we are so that we can be even more effective instruments of His will. Don't cower from learning your weaknesses or leaving what you know to work in an area that's unfamiliar. God is only showing them to you because He knows that in your sequel, you will overcome those obstacles to shine even brighter. In changing companies from Overbrook to Edmonds to MGM to Sony, I have been following God's lead far out of my comfort zone, and I have learned much about who I am, how I need to grow, and what I can do to be better at my work. The learning curve has been steep at times, but in the process I have received lessons that I now consider central to my work as an executive:

- *BE A FRIEND OF THE FILM.* Even though it's important to manage the administrative aspects of a film like budget and schedule, it's also important to be supportive of the creative process.

- *BE A COLLABORATOR AND PROBLEM SOLVER.* This goes hand in hand with being a friend of the film. My attitude with every movie I work on is "How can I help the team win?" If there's a problem, how can I help solve it? How can I facilitate others doing their best work?

- *I WILL GET OUT WHAT I PUT IN.* If I'm on a film, there's no aspect of that film, from the screenplay to the set design to the music to the casting, that I don't want to learn about. I might not be part of the decision-making process in some of those areas, but that's not the point. Understanding every aspect of what you do is important.

- *EVEN IF MY PART IN A PROJECT IS SMALL, GIVE IT EVERYTHING.* In an article called "Facing the Challenge of a New Age" in the *Phylon Quarterly*, Martin Luther King Jr. wrote, "If a man is called to be a street sweeper, he should sweep streets even as Michelangelo painted, or Beethoven composed music, or Shakespeare wrote poetry. He should sweep streets so well that all the hosts of heaven and earth will pause to say, here lived a great street sweeper who did his job well." There is honor and dignity in doing any job well.

- *DON'T BE AFRAID TO SPEAK UP.* People are people, regardless of stature, from movie stars to CEOs. You should respect their titles and positions in the world, but not let intimidation prevent you from speaking up. You have to have confidence in your point of view and not be afraid to share it. If you let fear rule you, you'll never have a sequel.

HAVE YOU EVER KNOWN anyone who was extremely successful at his or her career—making great money, doing interesting work—who suddenly left that career to do something completely different, like start a small business? Most of us have, and when we see that, we're witnessing the result of God whispering in that person's ear and sending them into the third kind of sequel.

The restlessness, ennui, or loss of passion that some people experience when they get too comfortable in their careers is placed in their hearts by God. He made us to strive and overcome obstacles, not to get complacent in work that only rewards us financially. We are meant to build and struggle and discover, and whenever someone's work does not grant him those blessings, after a while he will say, "Enough." God will place in his heart the desire to seek elsewhere for fulfillment, challenge, and passion. This is why so many of us have multiple careers in our lives. This is why wealthy CEOs leave million-dollar jobs to work with charities in Africa or successful performers quit in order to preach the Word. We need God's purpose to animate our work; without that, it becomes stale drudgery.

When too much success or too much routine robs our work of its vitality, God will fill us with the desire to start from scratch doing something that perhaps we wanted to do as a teenager but did not. In this regard, our generation has incredible spiritual potential. In centuries past, most people had few options. You did what your father and grandfather did for a living. You worked at the same shop or factory or farm and that was that. You could not change careers on a whim.

We no longer suffer such limitations in modern society. Many men and women have the resources and freedom to take their lives in a different direction should they so choose and will often do so multiple times in their lives. This is the age of entrepreneurship and global technology. Today, if we reach a point in our career where we are no longer driven to produce for God, he may call upon us to start over in a new line of work, or even create an entirely new line of work in order to produce our sequel.

This third type of sequel usually announces its coming with the boredom or dissatisfaction with a career that to this point had been perfectly fulfilling and satisfactory. According to *Fast Company* magazine, about 10 percent of the people who dream about making a radical career change actually do it. That's millions of Americans. Granted, some of them probably have no choice due to downsizing or relocation, but it still takes great faith and courage to listen to that small voice telling you to pursue the passion you've harbored since you were in college.

If a time comes (or has already come) when you feel that despite money, position, and status your work no longer matters or leaves you feeling as if you are missing your calling, God is placing his hand on your heart. He is placing those feelings within you because you have a higher purpose that is not being met by your current situation. When such feelings arise, be aware of them and bless them. Do not fear them, for they will always lead you in the direction of God's true mission.

GOD IS ALWAYS IN the plan. No matter what happens in your life, God has already directed a path for you. He wants you to keep moving forward and to rise above what you have already done. He has glory in store for you! That's an especially relevant fact to keep in mind in the terrible economy and job market. Every day I remind myself how blessed I am to be working in my field. I am keenly aware that many others are not so fortunate. Yet, I pray these words will encourage you if you find yourself in that category.

The fourth type of sequel comes when we lose our jobs due to layoff or the closure of our company, and it's the hardest scenario in which to see God's blessing. But that blessing is present.

If you have been suffering through unemployment, you may be saying, "Don't tell me about Development and Production. I can't even find a job so I can pay my bills." You could be wondering why God isn't helping you with your story. But here's the thing: *He is.* God is collaborating with you on your story right now! The plot may simply be taking a twist that you cannot understand at this time. No matter how hopeless things may seem, he always has a reason for each high and low point, and that reason will serve to bring you into production at the right place and time.

If you have lost your job, know that God still has a purpose for you and the next job you get will bring you closer to it. In a bad economy we might stick with a job that does not fire our passions out of a need for simple survival; we're afraid that if we quit we won't be able to find another job. But know the Lord will even use that temporary job to set you up for the next situation.

If you have been out of work for a long time, God is using this time in order to change you into a superior instrument for his will. Unemployment can be the process that polishes you until you gleam like a jewel, capable of great things in the future. Remember, God always takes the long view. Nothing shapes and strengthens us like difficulty, and nothing teaches perspective and gratitude like hard times. An extended period of economic privation may help you become more resourceful, kind, persistent, brave, and tolerant—all qualities that serve Christians well. Hard times will eventually give way to better times, but your spiritual development will remain with you for the rest of your life.

How can you take this downtime to help improve your craft? Aspiring actors work on skills they apply to their performances when they finally get new roles. Aspiring writers finish the screenplays they couldn't when they had nine-to-five jobs. Aspiring novelists write novels that have been rattling around in their heads since college. Use these tough times to reconnect with others and work on yourself as much as possible. For some, what began as harsh, frightening episodes turn out to be some of the most valuable periods of their lives—the periods that lead directly to their sequels.

Remember my friend Glendon? He came up with the idea for *Jumping the Broom* while he was unemployed. These downtimes are the very times God can use to plant ideas that will lead to your future success.

As Christians, we are taught to find the will and purpose of God in everything, even in events that seem to bring pain and misery. We must be mindful of the fact that even when times are dark, God's light is present. Right now, on this very day, he already has a plan to put you back into Development, bring you to Production, and then send you into your sequel. The way is already prepared. There is a reason for the economic upheaval we all face. There is hope. Your role in these dark times has a divine purpose that will reveal itself.

I WANT TO LEAVE you with a beautiful and stunning truth:

Just as you believe in God, God believes in you.

In fact, God believes in you even more strongly than you believe in yourself. He sees the end of your road and knows what you are capable of. He made you capable of rising to greatness. You may not ever produce or star in a Hollywood movie, but that doesn't matter. Your story is still one of the best ever told.

There is more hope in this than I can even express in words. The Lord is working right now, this very second, to create the next installment in your story. He is at work on your behalf right now! He is setting blessings in motion that will intersect your road at certain points; the more you trust him to lead you down the right roads (even if you don't think they are right), the more powerful and rewarding those blessings will be. No matter what kind of sequel you are in the middle of making, it will lead to greater joys if you keep the faith.

Following God doesn't mean everything will be okay all the time, or that if we follow him then we're going to get some proverbial pot of gold at the end of the rainbow. No, following God means that regardless of the difficulties we face along the way, it's all about the journey. In that our faith will make us successful.

To whom much is given, much is required. God asks much of us, and if we give it willingly, he will give us everything we have dreamed of. Stay true to your commitment to the values in your work. Pursue purpose before money. Create value for your employer and for those with whom you work. Be proud of your faith before colleagues and superiors. Demonstrate what it means to be a Christian through deeds of fairness and honor, generosity and humility. By doing these things, even if you do not feel as if you are in God's purpose today in your work, trust me, you are.

Opportunities will appear ready for your ideas and vision to make them come alive. People will enter your life, bringing relationships and access to what you need. God is always in the plan. God *is* the plan. He will *never* fail to do his part. When God is producing your life by faith, you don't have to fear what comes next in your movie. Fear is what keeps us stuck and keeps us from our purpose. God has made you equal to every challenge he will bring before you.

God wants us to reach out and grasp the joy and opportunity to be found in a career and life that are committed to him. He has validated that for me; everything I have accomplished has been a combination of God lining it up and me pursuing it. I've found my passion and he's blessed me by surrounding me with many people who could help me bring it to fruition. They could have laughed me out of the room when I asked a dumb question or said the wrong thing, but they didn't. God has always put me where he needed me to be.

God has made you ready for anything. Take the initiative. Go out on a limb. Make the first move. No one but God can define who or what you are. When you step out in faith, he will bring you opportunities and purpose that surpass even your wildest expectations.

Then, when the end credits of your life roll and everyone wonders how you did it, you won't have to say a word. All you'll have to do is point to the screen and it will say, *Produced by Faith.*

- What do you think your sequel might be?

- Which kind of sequel does God have you working on and why?

- Have you had cause to reinvent your career? What did you do?

- Have you spent a long period of time out of work?

- What did you learn during that time? What new skills did you develop? In what way was it a blessing for you?

- What are you doing to overcome your fear of pursuing the career of your dreams?

ACKNOWLEDGMENTS

The Bible says, "In everything give thanks; for this is the will of God in Christ Jesus for you." I am deeply humbled by the many people God has blessed me with to help bring this idea to life.

My Lord and Savior, Jesus Christ: thank you, for without you, none of this would be possible.

Jonathan Merkh, Becky Nesbitt, Holly Halverson, and the amazing Howard Books and Simon & Schuster staff: thank you for believing in me. This has been a phenomenal, life-changing experience.

Tim Vandehey: you are a master at your craft. Without you it would have been impossible to get this message out of me. Thank you for letting God use you in a mighty way. I'm grateful that he thought enough of me to bring you into my life.

Jillian Manus: you are not just my agent but also my angel. I'll never forget when you looked at me and told me this was something I must do. Thank you for seeing something in me that I didn't see in myself.

Amy Pascal and Michael Lynton: thank you for your visionary leadership and for creating an environment that makes Sony one of the best places to work in the world.

Doug Belgrad: thank you for being the example; you wrote the book on excellence. I'm blessed to be on your team.

Matt Tolmach: thank you for helping me find my creative voice as an executive.

Elizabeth Cantillon: *thank you* seems like an understatement—I'd be absolutely nowhere without you. You are an inspiration. Thank you for your faith and unwavering support. I have no idea what I'd do without you, and I'm glad I'll never have to know.

Hannah Minghella: thank you for your leadership, creative passion, and our friendship. I appreciate you.

Ange Giannetti: you are an amazing teacher and friend. You have taught me so much, and I'm forever grateful for you.

Sam Dickerman, Rachel O'Connor, Jonathan Kadin, Adam Milano, Lauren Abrahams, Karen Moy, Andrew Dodge, and my entire Columbia and Sony Pictures family: few are fortunate to work with colleagues as gifted and amazing as you. Thank you from the bottom of my heart for making every day a true joy.

Peter Schlessel: thank you for your guidance and wisdom.

Will Smith and Jada Pinkett Smith: I'm blessed to have you in my life. You inspire to me to make everything I touch better. I pray that everyone who touches this book will be impacted by the influence you have had on my life. Thank you for setting the standard.

James Lassiter: I'm thankful for all you have done for me. It's a blessing to be able to apply all that I've learned from you not just to make good movies but to help people improve their lives.

Ken Stovitz: thank you for being such a tremendous mentor and dear friend.

Miguel Melendez: thank you, homey, for your advice, support, and friendship. You were a key part of helping shape the vision for this book. Thank you for letting God speak through you.

Jana Babatunde-Bey and all of Overbrook Entertainment: thank you, you are my family; I love each and every one of you.

Tracey E. Edmonds: thank you for giving me a shot. You came through for me in a moment when I needed it most. I'm grateful for our friendship and thankful for your presence in my life.

Drew Fitzgerald and Alan Silfen: you are creative geniuses. The cover is incredible. Thank you for sacrificing your time to help me bring this vision to life.

Pastor D. J. Williams, Aunt Ida, and my Wings of Love family: so much of who I have become is because of you. You are my rock and my foundation. Your love keeps me going. Because of your sacrifice, I am here today; thank you for showing me what faith is all about.

Bishop T.D. Jakes and First Lady Serita Jakes: thank you for inspiring my life in such a dynamic and profound way. I am a seed that your word has helped nurture and grow. I still can't believe how God brought us together, and I'm grateful that I can play a role in getting your message to the world.

Pastor Joel Osteen and Victoria Osteen: your kindness and love have meant more to me than you know. Thank you for your support and divine friendship.

Pastor Michael Kelly, Tia Kelly, and my Mt. Rubidoux

family: I love you all. God is moving through you in a powerful way. Thank you for your vision and for helping me grow in ministry.

To my mentors in ministry Servant Brian K. Woodson, Sr., Dr. Jerome Crichton, Apostle Bam Crawford, Pastor Wayne Chaney, Pastor William Dawson, and Brother Alvin Clavon Sr.: thank you for your guidance and support.

To my brothers, Donald Ray Franklin II and Pastor David Brandon Franklin: I love you and I couldn't have done this without you. We've stuck together and succeeded against all the odds. Thank you for showing me the way; I'd be lost without you.

To my cousins Trent and Tashena: thank you for helping me enjoy the essence of life—your laughter and love keep me going.

To my cousin Staci: thank you for always having my back.

To Aunt Donna: thank you for teaching me what life is all about—I live by these lessons every day. Thank you for being there for me; I love you dearly.

Aunt Sondra and David Glover: thank you for being my professional genesis. Your commitment to the community has influenced me and OCCUR has helped shaped me into the person and executive I am today.

To Aunt Nuna, Aunt Jayne, Aunt Chrystal, and Aunt Enis: thank you for loving me and never giving up on me. I'm here today because of you. Thank you for wrapping me in your love. I love you.

To all my many aunts, uncles, and cousins: I am nothing without you. You are my family and I'm grateful for each and every one of you. Thank you for your support; you are my heart.

To all my friends: each one of you is a vibrant piece of the quilt God has used to create who I am. Thank you for making my life better.

To my mom, Paulette Franklin: words cannot express how much I love and appreciate you. You are a real-life superwoman, and I marvel at your strength. You are my hero: when life got tough you put your cape around Ray, Brandon, and me; you flew us to safety and protected us from danger. Thank you for saving me. Thank you for your sacrifice. I love you eternally. This is for you.